THE
SCOTTISH
KITCHEN

The National Trust
for Scotland

THE
SCOTTISH
KITCHEN

CHRISTOPHER TROTTER

AURUM PRESS

For Henry and Byam

Thanks to:
Jonathan and Jenny White for letting us use Myres Castle for photography,
All the staff at Myres Castle,
Everyone at Falkland Palace,
Ninian Crichton Stuart and family for recipes,
Lorna Hepburn of the Tenement House,
The Lorimer family for recipes,
Bruce Bennet and everyone at the Pillars of Hercules,
Gregor McMaster for help with research,
Olive Geddes at the National Library of Scotland,
Carolyn Scott,
and of course my wife Caroline.

First published 2004 by Aurum Press Limited,
25 Bedford Avenue, London WC1B 3AT.

Text copyright © 2004 by Christopher Trotter.

Christopher Trotter has asserted his right to be identified as
the author of this book in accordance with the Copyright
Designs and Patents Act 1988.

All photographs are by Gary Baker except those on pages 6, 89
and 144 which are copyright © The National Trust for Scotland.

The National Trust for Scotland logo copyright © 2004
by The National Trust for Scotland

A copyright record for the book is available from The British Library.

ISBN 1 85410 979 0

Book design by Robert Updegraff.
Printed in Italy by Printer Trento.

Title spread: *Roast grouse with celeriac purée and brambles.*
Overleaf: *The Vegetable Garden at Inverewe.*

CONTENTS

INTRODUCTION

The National Trust for Scotland is a charity which preserves and conserves its properties as well as making them accessible to visitors who come and learn about our heritage. This book tries to do the equivalent for food by giving a glimpse of Scottish food and cooking as it was in the past and as it is today. Some of the recipes have been passed down through families who have lived in Trust properties, the Lorimers at Kellie Castle, Ninian Crichton Stuart and his sisters in Falkland Palace. I have also researched recipes from periods particularly associated with some of the properties, and have read the recipe books of the Malcolm family, now in the National Library of Scotland, which cover a span of 100 years in the seventeenth and eighteenth centuries. I have also obtained recipe ideas from the cooks working in the tea rooms and restaurants in The National Trust for Scotland properties today.

Scotland is a country with a long tradition of food preservation and cooking. From the first, food would have been cooked in big pots over a constantly burning peat fire. In France the tradition is called *pot au feu* or 'pot over the fire'. I call it 'All in the pot' cooking and many of the great dishes stem from this idea of cooking everything together in a single pot. Some of our best known dishes have been devised to make the best of produce which would, in the past, have been preserved out of necessity but is now salted, smoked or otherwise treated because, over the centuries, we have acquired a taste for it, examples are kippers, Arbroath smokies, smoked salmon or the salted and smoked haddock which goes into dishes such as Cullen Skink.

Scotland has a huge natural resource not just from the hills and lochs with their deer and trout, but from the sea which has always provided an abundance of fish and shellfish. Whole communities, such as Ullapool in the north west and the East Neuk villages of Fife in the east, have grown up on the shores of good fishing grounds. There is also a great tradition of husbandry, Scotland has a long, slow growing season and the farmers have learned to work with and not against the natural constraints of soil and climate; as a result we now have some of the finest raw produce in the world.

Scotland is synonymous with quality - producing world-famous beef, lamb, soft fruits, salmon and lobster. If you look closer you will find that, as in France, there is a regional feel to much of our food, and whilst today dishes which originate from specific places are served all over the country, I have tried to show which regions are responsible for producing certain foods or dishes and why.

Christopher Trotter, Upper Largo, 2004.

Soups
and
Starters

BAKED EGGS TENTSMUIR

(from Fife)

I am very fond of egg dishes like this and relish their simplicity. The eggs must be very good, with rich yolks; organic ones are the best.

Chanterelles can be found growing wild in Scotland during August, September and October. Tentsmuir Forest is on the northern side of the River Eden and can be seen from St Andrews. As a child I enjoyed many walks there with my family, both on the wonderful long beach and in the forest itself. After I got married we would go there as a family and cook barbecues on the dunes, usually venison sausages. We also enjoyed local strawberries and wonderful Scotch eggs, which my wife prepared with the children. However, it is the fungi that can be found among the trees that I most vividly remember from my youth – there were ceps and puff balls, but mainly chanterelles. My mother would show us how to look for them under the moss and how to search and collect without damaging the ground too much. This recipe is simplicity itself, but with such flavours who needs to do much? It comes from a well known Fife hotelier, Peter Aretz.

Makes 10
Preparation time: 15 mins

300g (10oz) bacon, diced
butter, for greasing
150g (5oz) chanterelles, finely chopped
1 tbsp fresh chopped herbs such as parsley,
    chervil, or tarragon

salt and freshly ground black pepper
10 eggs

1   Preheat the oven to 200°C (400°F/Gas 6).

2   Fry the bacon until crisp. Divide among 10 buttered ramekin dishes. Add the chanterelles. Sprinkle with herbs, season lightly, and break a raw egg on top of each.

3   Bake in the oven until the eggs have just set.

BAKED GOAT'S CHEESE PARCEL WITH A ROCKET SAUCE

(from Dumfries)

Serves 4
Preparation time: 20 mins

115g (4oz) puff pastry
flour, for dusting
4 goat's cheese crottins, sliced
1 egg mixed with a little milk

For the sauce:
handful of rocket (arugula)
1 clove garlic
1 spring onion (scallion)
3 tbsp olive oil
12 black olives, pitted
squeeze of lemon juice

1   Preheat the oven to 220°C (425°F/Gas 7).

2   Roll out the pastry on a lightly floured board and create 4 squares large enough to take 1 crottin with the slices stacked against each other. Brush the egg wash all around them and bring the diagonal corners of the pastry to meet in the middle, then pinch them together, leaving gaps at the sides.

3   Put all the sauce ingredients in a food processor and whiz to form a purée.

4   Bake the crottin parcels in the oven until brown, puffed and bubbling; drizzle the sauce over and around, and serve.

DUMFRIES, GALLOWAY AND ARRAN

What a diverse region this is. Historically the Clyde Valley was the vegetable garden for Glasgow, and in the 1970s there was a huge tomato industry, which was all but destroyed by the rise in the price of oil for heating the glasshouses in which the fruit were grown. But today the Clyde tomato is making a return with a flavour and colour superior to any imported from the Canaries or across the North Sea.

Historically, cheese-making was a skill carried on in farms all over Scotland, a tradition decimated by the Second World War, during which all milk production was commandeered and cheese-making centrally managed to ensure a healthy national diet. Afterwards, when the old skills had been forgotten, cheese-making was taken over by the Milk Marketing Board. Apart from English or imported cheese, all we had were bland Dunlop-style cheeses. It was in this region, at the College of Agriculture in Auchencruive, that Scottish artisan cheese-making was first revived, with the result that, in this region alone, there are now many cheese-makers, such as Ann Dorward, Barry Graham and, on Arran, Iain Macleary, and the industry is spreading to other regions, where practitioners include Humphrey Errington, near Biggar, and of course the Reade family on the Isle of Mull, whose enterprise merits a chapter to itself.

Scotland has some of the finest cheese-makers in Britain, but cheese is not the only product of the Scottish dairy industry; our ice cream is also excellent and in this region the Cream O' Galloway company has been making superb ice cream for a number of years now. It is not just the revived traditions that make these products good, it is also the quality of the pasture, and hence the milk.

There is also a great tradition of beef-rearing here, with the familiar 'beltie' the best-known breed, and there is also Ayrshire bacon, which refers more to the method of production than the area of origin. In Carluke the Ramsay brothers produce a superb dry-cured bacon which discerning shoppers are seeking out across Scotland.

Arran, the island off the Ayrshire coast, has in recent years experienced a revolution in its food production. As well as the cheese-making which I have referred to, there is a small salad and herb grower, and an excellent smokehouse. So don't just visit Brodick Castle – search out the food producers as well.

Unpasteurized cow's milk, goat's milk and ewe's milk cheeses,
all products of the revival of artisan cheese-making in Scotland.

BELLEVUE BLUE AND PINE NUT SALAD

(from Dumfries)

I cannot mention a salad recipe without taking the opportunity to reintroduce
Mary Malcolm's recipe for salad dressing which I found in the National
Library of Scotland.

*Take some leaves cut into convenient pieces Yolks of 2 hard boiled eggs, tsp French
mustard, pepper and salt, tablespoon of oil work into a smooth paste add
consecutively 3 tablespoons of oil 1 of tarragon and 1 of plain vinegar, then
chopped chervil garden cress and tarragon.*

I love the expression 'convenient pieces'. But her recipe shows that quite a lot
of herbs were available in the late eighteenth century.

Blue cheese is always good in a dressing, but this salad uses the Arran blue
cheese as part of the salad. The combination of the toasted nuts and sweet figs
makes a lovely first course.

Serves 4
Preparation time: 20 mins

4 tsp pine nuts
mixed salad leaves, including rocket (arugula)
   and lollo rosso
4 fresh figs
115g (4oz) crumbled Bellevue blue cheese

For the dressing:
3 tbsp peanut oil
juice of 1 lemon
salt and freshly ground black pepper
pinch of caster (superfine) sugar

1 Toast the pine nuts under a hot grill (broiler) or dry toast them in a hot pan with no fat,
until they are light brown.

2 Tear the salad leaves into bite-sized pieces and toss them together in a bowl to create a
mass of colours.

3 Mix all the dressing ingredients and add to the salad leaves; toss to mix thoroughly.

4 Wipe the figs and cut into quarters but without cutting through, so they open up
showing the beautiful pink interior. Arrange on the salad leaves.

5 Sprinkle over the cheese and finally sprinkle the pine nuts over the top.

BREAST OF PIGEON WITH PUY LENTILS

(from Fife)

The rich flavour of the pigeon is complemented by the earthy flavour of the
lentils and this is a dish you can develop to your own liking, adding chopped
onions or celery or mushrooms just after adding the bacon strips. They can all
add flavour and texture to the basic dish. Go on – experiment!

Serves 4
Preparation time: 15 mins

450g (1lb/2 ¹/₂ cups) Puy lentils
a little oil and butter, for frying
4 pigeon breast fillets (halves)
4 slices smoked bacon

1 clove garlic, crushed
300ml (10fl oz/¹/₂ cup) stock
salt and freshly ground black pepper
a little extra butter (optional)

1   Wash and drain the lentils; simmer in a large pan of water for about 10 minutes to
    soften slightly. Drain and set aside.

2   Melt the butter with the oil in a large frying pan and, when hot, place the pigeon breasts
    in it, skin side down. Cook on a high heat for 2 or 3 minutes to seal in the juices, turn
    them over, and repeat on the other side. Cover the pan and lower the heat and cook
    gently for 5 minutes. Remove the breasts and keep them warm.

3   Cut the bacon into lardons, strips about 2cm (³/₄ in) long, and fry in the pan until
    lightly coloured, add the garlic and cook briefly. Add the lentils and stir to coat in the
    pan juices.

4   Add the stock and simmer until nearly evaporated, leaving a rich broth texture to the
    lentils. Check the seasoning. If you like, swirl in some cold chunks of butter to enrich it
    still more. Serve by making pools of lentils with a breast on top or slice each breast
    lengthwise first and place on top.

FENNEL AND STRATHDON BLUE SOUP

(from Highlands)

This excellent cheese from Aberdeenshire goes very well with the aniseedy
flavour of the fennel. It is the bulb you use for the soup; the fabulous fronds
go very well with fish.

Serves 4
Preparation time: 20 mins

25g (1oz/2 tbsp) butter
3 bulbs fennel, washed and roughly chopped
2 leeks, white parts only, chopped
125g (4 oz) potatoes, peeled and chopped
550ml (20fl oz/2¹/₂ cups) chicken stock

freshly ground black pepper
150ml (5fl oz/²/₃ cup) milk
115g (4 oz) Strathdon blue cheese
150ml (5fl oz/²/₃ cup) single (light) cream

1   In a large pan, melt the butter and sweat the fennel and leek in the butter until
    softened; do not allow to colour.

2   Add the potatoes and mix together to coat in the butter. Add the stock, bring to the boil
    and simmer gently until the potatoes are soft. Season with pepper and add the milk and
    cheese; return to the boil and remove from the heat.

3   Allow to cool a little and then liquidize. Stir in the cream, check for seasoning, and serve.

Caramelized Onion Tart

(from Dumfries)

Serves 4
Preparation time: 1 hour

5 large onions
115g (4oz/ $^1/_2$ cup) butter
150ml (5fl oz/ $^2/_3$ cup) double (heavy) cream

salt and freshly ground black pepper
2 eggs, beaten
250g (9oz) shortcrust pastry

1 Peel and finely chop the onions; try to keep them as even a size as possible as this gives the dish uniformity.

2 Melt the butter in a large frying pan, which you can also cover enough to keep some heat in. Add the onions and sweat them over a high heat, then stir around in the butter; cover the pan and allow onions to exude some steam. After 4 minutes remove the lid and reduce the heat a little.

3 Continue to cook gently, stirring occasionally, for up to 45 minutes; this allows the natural sugar to come out. When the onions begin to colour light brown, pour in the cream and allow to simmer for a few minutes to thicken, then remove the pan from the heat and add salt and pepper. When cool, mix in the eggs.

4 Preheat the oven to 220°C (425°F/Gas 7).

5 Roll out the pastry and line a 20cm (8in) metal flan case with it; bake blind for about 20 minutes. When the pastry is cool, pour in the onion mixture and bake in the oven for 15 minutes until set and lightly browned.

6 Serve hot or warm on its own for a first course or with a salad for a light supper dish.

Cullen Skink Soup

(from Aberdeen)

This traditional soup is still served in the café at Crathes Castle where Alison
Mitchell is the cook. The blend of smoked haddock with milk and potato creates
a wonderfully smooth soup and reflects so much of what Scottish food is about –
good, natural ingredients, simply prepared to create something delicious.

Serves 4
Preparation time: 45 mins

450g (1lb) undyed smoked haddock fillets
900ml (32fl oz/4 cups) milk
1 bay leaf
1 onion, peeled and sliced

1 potato, peeled and chopped
freshly ground black pepper
2 tsp chopped fresh parsley

1 In a large pan, place the fish, milk and the bay leaf, and poach gently over a low heat or
   the milk will burn; it only takes a few minutes.

2 Remove the fish and add the onion and potato to the milk and continue to cook gently
   until soft. When the vegetables are soft, remove and discard the bay leaf.

3 Liquidize the potato and milk mixture to a smooth cream. (A food processor is not good
   enough; you need to use a liquidizer.) When ready, return the liquidized mixture to the
   pan and season with pepper.

4 Flake the smoked fish back into the soup and serve with the chopped parsley sprinkled
   over.

FEATHER FOWLIE

(from Highlands)

Based on the chicken-in-the-pot idea, this recipe uses bacon for flavour and is enriched with eggs and cream. You can either use a chicken carcass with a few bits still on or legs and winglets and get more meat off them after the initial cooking.

Serves 4
Preparation time: 1 hour

25g (1oz/2 tbsp) butter
75g (2 ¹/₂ oz) bacon, chopped
1 stalk celery, sliced
1 onion, sliced
1 carrot, sliced
2 joints (quarters) of chicken or a carcass, wings etc
1 litre (35fl oz/4¹/₂ cups) water
herb stalks and bay leaf
chopped fresh herbs

For the liaison:
1 egg yolk
100ml (3fl oz/scant ¹/₂ cup) single (light) cream
salt and freshly ground black pepper

1   In a large pan, melt the butter and sweat the bacon in the butter for a few minutes. Add the vegetables, and cook, stirring, until they soften.

2   Add the chicken; if you are using the carcass then let it colour a little, if using joints allow to cook. Add the water, the herb stalks and bay leaf. Simmer for about 1 hour 15 minutes.

3   Remove and discard the herbs stalks and bay leaf. Remove the chicken, and when cool enough, remove the meat from the bone and return it to the soup. Liquidize the soup with the chicken meat and return to the heat.

4   Mix the liaison ingredients together and blend with a little of the hot soup, return the egg mixture to the pan and heat through but do not boil; the soup will thicken slightly. Add lots of fresh herbs, check for seasoning, and serve.

HOTCHPOTCH

(from Highlands)

A spring version of the classic Scotch broth, still using the tough bits of the lamb but with the freshness of young vegetables.

Serves 4
Preparation time: 3 hours

3 carrots, diced
6 spring onions (scallions), chopped
1kg (2 ¼ lb) neck of lamb
3 litres (105fl oz/13 cups) water
bouquet garni
4 small white turnips, diced

1 small cauliflower, broken into florets
115g (4oz) broad (fava) beans
115g (4oz) fresh or frozen green peas
2 little gem lettuce, shredded
2 tbsp chopped fresh parsley
salt and freshly ground black pepper

1   When preparing the vegetables reserve the peelings from the carrots and spring onions (scallions).

2   Put the neck of lamb and water in a large pan to make the stock; add the reserved vegetable peelings and bouquet garni to flavour it. Simmer for about 2 hours. Strain off the liquid, and when the lamb is cool enough to handle, remove the meat and cut into chunks, then set aside.

3   Meanwhile, return the stock to the heat, add the carrots and turnips, and simmer for 5 minutes. Add the cauliflower and simmer for a further 5 minutes. Add the beans, followed by the peas and spring onions (scallions) a few minutes later.

4   Return the soup to the boil, add the diced meat, lettuce, and chopped parsley, and check the seasoning. Result – bowl of fresh crunchy vegetables with a rich lamb stock!

Langoustines with Tomato and Saffron Sauce

(from Argyll)

Serves 4 (or 6 as a starter)
Preparation time: 1 hour 30 mins

20 live langoustines (large prawns), about 1kg (2lb 4oz)
1 tsp sea salt
1 tbsp olive oil
1 shallot, peeled and chopped

pinch of saffron threads
4 tbsp dry white wine
450g (1lb) fresh ripe tomatoes, roughly chopped, or canned equivalent

1   Fill a large pan, which will easily hold the prawns, with water and bring it to the boil. Add the sea salt and throw in the prawns. If necessary, do it in two batches. Let the prawns come back to the boil then drain through a colander so they can dry off.

2   When they are cool, reserve 4 whole prawns (choose the best ones with two claws!). Shell the remaining prawns: first break off the tails and the heads, then peel the shells away from the prawns, taking care to keep them intact. Reserve the heads, tails and shells.

3   In a large sauté or frying pan, heat the olive oil, add the shallot and allow to sweat gently for a few minute without colouring. Stir in the saffron and then throw in all the shellfish debris, stirring to coat with saffron. Using a wooden spoon, break up the heads a bit to help bring out the flavour.

4   Add the wine, allow to bubble, then add the tomatoes and reduce the heat. Stir until the tomatoes soften and cook – about 5 minutes. If it becomes too dry, add some water. When soft, strain through a fine sieve into another pan and keep it warm; the sauce should be of a light broth texture.

5   To serve, warm the prawns in the sauce then pour the sauce into 4 white bowls or plates. Divide the prawns between the bowls, arranging them carefully in the sauce, and put one whole prawn on top of each serving.

LORRAINE SOUP

(from Edinburgh)

This soup is named after Mary of Lorraine, the wife of King James V whose daughter was Mary, Queen of Scots.

Serves 4
Preparation time: 1 hour

25g (1oz/2 tbsp) butter
25g (1oz/¼ cup) flour
1 litre (35fl oz/4½ cups) chicken stock
2 cooked chicken breast fillets (halves), finely chopped or minced (ground)
finely grated zest of 1 lemon

grated nutmeg
1 egg yolk
125ml (4½ fl oz/½ cup) single (light) cream
25g (1oz/¼ cup) ground almonds
salt and freshly ground black pepper

1 In a large pan, melt the butter and make a white roux with the butter and flour. Add the stock. Bring to the boil and simmer gently for 5 minutes.

2 Add the chopped chicken, lemon zest and nutmeg.

3 Whisk the egg yolk into the cream and add a ladleful of hot soup to it. Add the ground almonds and whisk together.

4 Return the almond mixture to the hot soup, stirring constantly until it comes almost to the boil, but do not allow it to boil or it will curdle. Adjust the seasoning and serve.

NETTLE SOUP

(from Highlands)

It is best to collect your nettles in the early season when they are still young and tender; just take the tops and not the tough stalks. The use of rubber gloves is a good idea for obvious reasons. Give the nettle leaves a good wash before use. It is likely that nettles have been used for centuries, not just for soup but as a vegetable as well. They also make an interesting infusion, and, like spinach, are packed full of minerals.

Serves 4
Preparation time: 50 mins

50g (2oz/¹/₂ cup) butter
1 onion, peeled and sliced
3 potatoes, peeled and sliced
550ml (20fl oz/2¹/₂ cups) vegetable or chicken stock

grated nutmeg
150g (5oz) young nettles (tops of plants only)
salt and freshly ground black pepper

1   Melt the butter in a heavy-based pan, add the onion and sweat gently until soft.

2   Add the potatoes, coating with the butter and heating through. Cover with the stock and simmer until the onion and potatoes are cooked. Season with nutmeg.

3   Add the nettles and cook briefly until they wilt; remove from the heat and leave to cool a little. Liquidize the soup, return it to the heat and check the seasoning. Like many soups, nettle soup tastes better if left overnight.

ORCADIAN OATMEAL

(from Highlands)

A very simple vegetable broth which uses oatmeal to provide the thickening. Depending on how you want it you can either roughly chop the vegetables and liquidize everything, or cut the vegetables as suggested here and keep a coarse texture; it's up to you. I personally like the bits! Do use a fine oatmeal as it takes less time to cook, but don't use rolled oats or it will taste like porridge!

Serves 4
Preparation time: 1 hour

50g (2oz/¹/₄ cup) butter
2 carrots, grated
1 leek, finely chopped
¹/₄ turnip, chopped into small dice

115g (4oz/1 cup) fine oatmeal (not rolled oats)
550ml (20fl oz/2¹/₂ cups) white stock
salt and freshly ground black pepper
550ml (20fl oz/2¹/₂ cups) milk

1   Melt the butter in a large pan and add all the vegetables. Stir over a low heat, cover, and allow to sweat for about 5 minutes.

2   Add the oatmeal and stir gently for another few minutes to absorb the buttery juices. Then add the stock, salt and pepper, and simmer for 15 minutes.

3   If you prefer a smooth soup, you can liquidize it, otherwise keep the texture of the vegetables; add the milk just before serving.

Salad of Rabbit with Wild Sorrel

(from Fife)

Wild sorrel, the natural diet of a wild rabbit, grows all over the place in
Scotland. It is also cultivated and you can buy it in supermarkets, but the tangiest
leaves are picked on a walk. Make sure you pick stuff just away from the path,
especially if it is used by dog walkers! And wash it well when you get home.

Serves 4
Preparation time: 30 mins

1 tbsp peanut oil (arachide)
2 saddles of rabbit, about 225g (8oz) each
salt and freshly ground black pepper
mixed salad leaves

handful of sorrel leaves
dressing (see page 14, Bellevue Blue and Pine
    Nut Salad)

1   Heat a heavy-based pan and add the oil. Dry the rabbit saddles and season them. Place
    in hot oil back-side down, and brown gently for about 4 minutes.

2   Turn them over, reduce the heat, cover, and cook very gently for about 5 minutes.

3   Remove the pan from the heat and let the meat rest for 5 minutes. Cut the fillets off the
    top of the bone and slice them thinly lengthwise, then cut out the small fillets
    underneath.

4   Mix the salad leaves and most of the sorrel with the dressing and place the warm rabbit
    slices on top; finish with a few sorrel leaves to garnish.

POTTED HOUGH

(from Glasgow)

Another product of one-pot cooking. This is simply well-cooked meat chopped into small pieces and set in a jelly formed from its own cooking juices. The cheaper cuts of meat, usually beef such as shin or flank, make excellent jellied stocks due to the gelatinous quality of some of the meat. I give here a basic recipe with just the hough (shin) and vegetables, but you can develop the theme by adding other cuts of meat, or a chicken carcass which has been browned in the oven along with its giblets.

Serves 6 or 8
Preparation time: 1 hour 30 mins + cooking time

1.5kg (3lb 4oz) shin of beef, cut through by
   your butcher
1 whole leek, untrimmed
1 large carrot
1 stalk celery
1 onion, peeled and stuck with 6 cloves

2 cloves garlic, crushed
2 bay leaves
sprig of thyme
8 peppercorns
parsley stalks
salt and freshly ground black pepper

1 Put the meat into a large pan and cover with water. Bring to the boil and skim off any froth or impurities that come to the surface.

2 Add the rest of the ingredients except the salt and pepper, and simmer for 4 or 5 hours or until the meat falls off the bone. Alternatively, cook it in the oven if you prefer at 180°C (350°F/Gas 4). Once cooked, remove the meat and set aside.

3 Strain the liquid into a clean pan and simmer until reduced by half. Remove from the heat, allow to cool, and refrigerate. The stock should become slightly jellied.

4 Chop the meat roughly into small pieces and place it in another pan. Add just enough of the stock to barely cover.

5 Bring to a boil and simmer gently for 5 minutes, then season with salt and pepper.

6 Wet 6 individual dariole moulds of about 150ml (5fl oz/²/₃ cup) or 8 ramekins of about 100ml (3¹/₂ fl oz/scant ¹/₂ cup). Pour the meat mixture into the moulds and chill thoroughly. To unmould, dip the moulds into warm water for a couple of minutes to melt the jelly slightly, then turn them out as you would a pâté.

PHEASANT BROTH

(from Highlands)

This is a good way to use up pheasant's legs if you have decided to use only the breasts of the birds in another dish. You can stockpile them in the freezer!

Serves 4
Preparation time: 4 hours

2 carcasses from cooked pheasants
2 litres (70fl oz/9 cups) brown stock
3 leeks, chopped
2 carrots, peeled and chopped
1 head of celery, chopped
1 onion, peeled and stuck with cloves
1 bay leaf

sprig each of thyme and rosemary
115ml (4fl oz/^{1}/$_2$ cup) sherry
salt and freshly ground black pepper
450g (1lb) diced pheasant meat, including leg meat
150ml (5fl oz/^{2}/$_3$ cup) Madeira
chopped fresh parsley (optional)

1   Preheat the oven to 220°C (425°F/Gas 7).

2   Chop up the pheasant carcasses, and brown them in the oven for about 30 minutes.

3   Remove the carcasses from the oven and place in a large saucepan with the stock, vegetables, bay leaf, thyme and rosemary. Bring to the boil and simmer slowly for about 2 hours, then strain off the liquid, pushing the vegetables through the strainer to give a good texture. Remove any pieces of meat that can be chopped and added to the final soup.

4   Allow the stock to cool and skim off the fat. Return the stock to a saucepan, add the sherry and simmer very gently for 30 minutes, then season. Add the diced meat and any meat retrieved from the stock. Finish with the Madeira and, if you like, some chopped parsley.

Salmon with Sorrel Cream Sauce

(from Argyll)

This is really a classic French recipe – *saumon a l'oseille*. We used to do a
version of the sauce with smoked haddock at the Savoy in London, which I
loved. Sorrel grows wild all over the place and I used to collect mine from the
shores of Loch Awe. The slightly astringent taste of sorrel, or 'sourrocks', as
we called it in Aberdeenshire, is a perfect foil for the texture and rich flavour
of salmon. Do chop it by hand and don't use a food processor, as this tends to
bruise it and impair the flavour.

Serves 4
Preparation time: 45 mins

tail piece of fresh salmon (see step 1)
85g (3oz/^{1}/$_3$ cup) butter
30 sorrel leaves, finely chopped

150ml (5fl oz/^{2}/$_3$ cup) dry white wine
300ml (10fl oz/1^1/$_4$ cups) double (heavy) cream
lemon juice (optional)

1   Chill the salmon in the freezer for about 30 minutes. Cut very thin slices from the
    salmon, as you would from smoked salmon, so that you have 3 x 50g (2oz) slices per
    person.

2   In a wide, heavy-based pan, melt the butter and cook the salmon very gently, turning it
    over once; it will take about 30 seconds on each side. It looks quite attractive if you let it
    take on a little colour. Remove the salmon and keep it warm.

3   Stir the sorrel into the pan, add the wine, and reduce to about 2 tablespoons. Add the
    cream, stir, and allow to reduce until it coats the back of a spoon. Add a squeeze of
    lemon juice if you like.

4   Spoon the sauce on to serving plates and place the salmon carefully on top – it will look
    stunning!

RED PEPPER AND MUSSEL SOUP

(from Highlands)

Although red peppers are scarcely traditional Highland produce, they are now
readily available everywhere, and you will certainly find plenty of mussels in
the west coast sea lochs. This is a good soup to give someone who does not like
the idea of eating mussels as you can purée them through the mixer,
or not, according to taste!

Serves 4
Preparation time: 1 hour

1kg (2¼ lb) fresh mussels
dash of white wine (optional)
2 tbsp olive oil
12 cloves garlic, peeled and sliced

4 large red (bell) peppers, seeded and chopped
850ml (30fl oz/3¾ cups) water
1 tsp sea salt

1 Clean the mussels by scrubbing well in cold water and, using a sharp knife, scrape them
to remove the 'beards'. Discard any broken ones and ones which do not close when
tapped sharply on the shell. Stew them in their own juices in a covered pan, with perhaps
a dash of white wine, until the shells open. Strain the mussels, reserving the liquor.

2 Heat the olive oil in another pan, and add the garlic; sweat it gently with the peppers
without colouring until soft – about 15 minutes. Add the mussel liquor and allow to
simmer, then add the water and salt, bring to the boil and simmer for a few minutes. Set
aside.

3 Remove the mussels from the shells and then either liquidize them with the broth or
keep them separate and serve mixed through the liquidized broth.

SHORE CRAB BREE

(from Highlands)

The little green crabs that you can find off the west coast are too small
for much else than this kind of treatment. They have a delicious
intensity and great colour.

Serves 4
Preparation time: 2 hours

1kg (2¹/₄ lb) small green shore crabs
50g (2oz/¹/₄ cup) butter
50g (2oz) each of onion, carrot, and celery,
   peeled and roughly chopped
2 tbsp Scotch whisky
5 very ripe tomatoes
1 tsp tomato purée
85ml (3fl oz/¹/₃ cup) white wine

1.7 litres (60fl oz/7¹/₂ cups) fish stock
sprig of tarragon
1 bay leaf
4 tbsp double (heavy) cream
salt and freshly ground black pepper
1 tsp lemon juice
paprika (optional)

1   Kill the crabs by plunging them into a large pan of boiling water for a couple of
minutes. Remove them to a large bowl and smash them with the end of a rolling pin.

2   In a heavy-based pan, melt the butter and sweat the vegetables in the butter for a while
to soften but not colour. Add the crabs and stir to really heat through. Add the whisky
and stir to steam the flavour through the crab. Add the tomatoes, tomato purée, wine,
stock, and the tarragon and bay leaf. Bring to the boil and simmer gently for about 40
minutes.

3   Strain the soup through a tough sieve, pushing through as much of the mixture as you
can. Alternatively, remove any big bits of claw and roughly whiz in a food processor, in
batches if necessary.

4   Return the soup to the heat and simmer for about 5 minutes to reduce a little and
intensify the flavour. Add the cream and check for seasoning. A little salt may be
needed but take care; add pepper, lemon juice, and perhaps a little paprika to taste.

Tomato, Basil and Goat's Cheese

(from Dumfries)

On the Isle of Arran they have a little micro-world of good things. There is an excellent little booklet called *The Arran Taste Trail* which gives details of many of the producers, growers and restaurants to be found on the island.

One of the notable eateries is at The National Trust for Scotland's property of Brodick Castle. The two main ingredients for the recipe both come from the Dumfries region, which includes the famous tomato-growing Clyde Valley and has excellent dairy herds creating some of Scotland's best cheeses, from Dunlop to Arran. I have chosen to use the little goat's crottin produced by an Arran cheese-maker, Ian Macleary, for this simple celebration of summer.

Serves 4
Preparation time: 30 mins

4 plump, ripe (Scottish) tomatoes
2 goat's cheese crottins
12 basil leaves

sea salt and freshly ground black pepper
extra-virgin olive oil

1   Preheat the grill (broiler).

2   Blanch and peel the tomatoes by plunging them into boiling water for 10 seconds then plunging them into cold water until completely cold. Take them out of the water and peel them. Thinly slice the tomatoes horizontally.

3   Thinly slice the crottins horizontally, or alternatively cut 3 slices from each and break each slice into two.

4   Arrange the tomato slices, basil leaves, and cheese slices in little piles on plates, seasoning each layer as you go. Sprinkle each plate with a good splurge of olive oil and flash under the grill (broiler) until the cheese starts to bubble. Serve immediately.

Twice-Baked Cheese Souffle

(from Dumfries; see photograph on back of jacket)

One of the most frequently requested recipes I ever do at demonstrations. The ease
of being able to slip a soufflé into the oven just before you need it is very attractive!
Normal cheese soufflés require a hard cheese like parmesan to give them flavour;
but this one, because it is baked twice, needs a softer type of cheese. A goat's crottin
from Arran (where else?) will do very well, or a soft cream cheese. It is a good dish to
do for a party because all the stress of the soufflé bit is done with before a guest is in
sight! I think it is best served and cooked the second time in small platters so they
can arrive undisturbed at the table with the sauce still bubbling!

Serves 12
Preparation time: 1 hour 30 mins

For the soufflés:
450ml (16fl oz/2 cups) milk
1 small onion
4 cloves
1 bay leaf
grated nutmeg
85g (3oz/¹/₃ cup) butter
85g (3oz/³/₄ cup) plain (all-purpose) flour
225g (8oz/1 cup) cream cheese
6 egg yolks
8 egg whites
pinch of salt

For the pesto:
150ml (5fl oz/²/₃ cup) virgin olive oil
50g (2oz/1 cup) fresh basil
1 tbsp pine nuts
1 clove garlic
salt
200ml (7fl oz/scant 1 cup) cream
50g (2oz/¹/₂ cup) grated Cheddar

1   Preheat the oven to 200°C (400°F/Gas 6).

2   Put the milk, the onion, spiked with the cloves, the bay leaf and nutmeg to taste in a pan
    and bring to the boil. Remove from the heat, cover and infuse for 10 minutes.

3   Melt the butter in a pan, add the flour and cook gently for 5 minutes. Remove from heat
    and strain the milk onto it, discard the onion and bay leaf. Return to a low heat and
    cook until thick, beating well. Add the cream cheese and beat until melted into the
    mixture.

4   Remove from the heat and beat in the egg yolks. Meanwhile, whisk the whites with a
    pinch of salt until stiff.

5 Add a quarter of the whites to the mixture and gently mix in, then return the mixture to the egg whites and fold through gently. Spoon the mixture into 12 ramekins lined with cling film (plastic wrap). Place in a tray of hot water and cook for about 15 minutes in the centre of the oven until lightly browned. Leave to cool. (At this stage, the soufflés can be refrigerated and kept for up to 1 week if you like.)

6 When ready to finish, turn out the soufflés and place in a suitable baking dish.

7 Increase the oven temperature to 220°C (425°F/Gas 7).

8 Place all the pesto ingredients in a blender except the cream and cheese and purée, then fold in the cream. Pour over soufflés and scatter with the grated cheese. Bake in the oven for about 15 minutes until lightly browned, risen, and bubbling. Lift the soufflés out of the baking dish and serve on individual plates.

TIMBALE OF COURGETTE WITH BONNET PESTO

(from Dumfries)

Serves 4
Preparation time: 1 hour 30 mins

3 courgettes (zucchini)
handful of fresh basil leaves
2 tbsp grated Bonnet cheese

2 cloves garlic
1 tbsp olive oil
salt and freshly ground black pepper

1 Preheat the oven to 200°C (400°F/Gas 6),

2 Trim the ends of the courgettes and cut into long thin strips. Blanch in boiling water until just soft, then refresh in cold water. Drain.

3 Put all the remaining ingredients into a food processor and whiz until well mixed to make a chunky pesto.

4 Line 4 ramekins with cling film (plastic wrap) leaving sufficient to cover the tops. Line them with the courgette strips so that they hang over the edge. Put a dollop of pesto in each and fold over the courgette strips to cover. Press down gently and cover with the cling film (plastic wrap). Cook gently in a bain marie (water bath) in the oven for 30 minutes.

5 Turn out carefully and serve with a tomato salsa (see page 154).

POACHED EGG WITH WILD GARLIC SAUCE

(from Fife)

The National Trust for Scotland's Kellie Castle in Fife has the most fantastic
wild garlic, which I am sure its former owners, the Lorimer family, will have
used. I actually cooked this recipe for a dinner party I once did at Kellie with
its tiny kitchen on two levels. I had to run up and down the spiral stairs in
between dishes and courses! However, like the proverbial swan, guests sitting
up in the beautiful hall were unaware of the frantic goings-on downstairs.
Wild garlic is also very good with lamb, and beef.

Serves 4
Preparation time: 30 mins

4 eggs
4 short-crust pastry tartlets, bought or made

If making yur own pastry, follow the
instructions given for Cullen Skink Tart
(page 42) but bake as four smaller tartlets
rather than the larger tart case.

For the garlic sauce:
1 tbsp white wine
2 egg yolks
175g (6oz/³/₄ cup) unsalted butter, melted
salt and freshly ground black pepper
14 wild garlic leaves
lemon juice to taste (optional)

1   In a stainless steel pan, make the sauce. Add the wine and egg yolks to the pan and
    whisk together over a low heat. When thickened slightly, keep whisking and remove
    from the heat.

2   Slowly add the melted butter, whisking all the time to form a thick liaison. Adjust the
    seasoning. Roll the garlic leaves into a cigar shape and slice them finely, then add to the
    sauce and stir in some lemon juice to taste if you like.

3   Poach the eggs and when ready remove from the water and drain carefully on kitchen
    paper (paper towels). Place in the pastry cases and spoon the sauce over; serve
    immediately.

FISH

Asparagus and Prawn Stirfry

(from Aberdeen)

This is an ideal recipe for the small asparagus, or sprue as it is called. Be quite ruthless when trimming them as you really only want the tips; the rest can go for soup. I very rarely suggest the use of frozen food, but in this instance I think the high quality of North Atlantic prawns is fine. They are best defrosted in advance and I always do this by tipping them into a colander or sieve to allow the water to drain away as they thaw, otherwise you can be left with a soggy mess!

Serves 4
Preparation time: 30 mins + thawing time

450g (1lb) frozen North Atlantic prawns, defrosted (see below)
450g (1lb) asparagus
2 tbsp peanut oil (arachide)

1 onion, peeled and finely chopped
1 tbsp toasted sesame seeds
3 tsp soy sauce
pinch of salt (may not be needed)

1   Defrost the prawns, see above.

2   Trim the asparagus so that you only have the tips; the remaining stalks can be used for making soup.

3   Heat a large, heavy-based pan until very hot, then add the peanut oil; throw in the chopped onion and stir quickly for a few minutes. Do not allow to colour too much.

4   Add the sesame seeds, then add the asparagus and a little water. This helps steam the asparagus. Finally add the soy sauce and mix together. Check for seasoning, and add salt if necessary. Serve with rice or noodles.

COD, SMOKED FISH AND KING SCALLOP PIE

(from Aberdeen)

Serves 4
Preparation time: 2 hours 30 mins

1kg (2lb) large, floury potatoes
a little milk and butter
1kg (2lb 4oz) cod fillet
225g (8oz) pale smoked fish
225ml (8fl oz/1 cup) milk
bay leaf
sprig fresh thyme
50g (2oz/¹/₂ cup) butter

25g (1oz/¹/₄ cup) plain (all-purpose) flour
grated nutmeg
100ml (3¹/₂ fl oz/scant ¹/₂ cup) dry vermouth
2 leeks, cut into 3cm (1¹/₄ in) lengths then in strips
8 king scallops, sliced in half across the centre
2 tsp each chopped fresh parsley and dill
freshly ground black pepper

1   Boil the potatoes in salted water until cooked, drain and return to the pan; return the
    pan to a low heat to dry a little. Add a little milk and butter which have been heated
    together to melt the butter. Mash the potatoes until smooth and creamy. Set aside.

2   Preheat the oven to 180°C (350°F/Gas 4).

3   Put the cod and smoked fish into a casserole dish with the milk, bay leaf, and thyme
    sprig, cover with foil and place in the oven for about 15 minutes. When just about cooked,
    remove from the milk and, when cooled a little, break the fish into flaky pieces.

4   Melt the butter in a pan and add the flour, then add the milk from the fish to form a
    smooth sauce; add a little grated nutmeg and the vermouth and stir in; cook gently for
    about 5 minutes.

5   Meanwhile, blanch the leeks in boiling water for 2 minutes and refresh in cold water;
    this just cooks them but keeps the colour. Drain thoroughly.

6   Add the leeks, the cooked fish, the raw scallops and the chopped herbs to the sauce;
    season with black pepper. Pour into a casserole and spread the mashed potato on top.
    Put the casserole in the oven for about 30 minutes until the top is lightly browned and it
    is hot through.

CULLEN SKINK TART

(from Aberdeen)

This is an idea developed from the cullen skink soup (see page 19) by
Alison Mitchell at Crathes, which, like the soup, she serves in the castle's café.

Serves 4
Preparation time: 2 hours

For the pastry:
225g (8oz/2 cups) plain (all-purpose) flour
pinch of salt
115g (4oz/½ cup) butter, sliced
1 egg, beaten

For the filling:
550ml (20fl oz/2½ cups) milk
150ml (5fl oz/⅔ cup) single (light) cream
2 egg yolks
pinch of chopped fresh thyme
2 fillets (about 200g/7oz) undyed, pale smoked
    haddock, cut into dice
200g (7oz) potatoes, peeled and diced
freshly ground black pepper

1   Preheat the oven to 200°C (400°F/Gas 6).

2   Sift the flour and the salt together into a bowl. Add the butter and rub into the flour
and salt until the mixture resembles fine breadcrumbs. Add the egg and mix to a light
dough. Cover in cling film (plastic wrap) and chill for about 20 minutes.

3   Roll the dough out on a lightly floured surface and line a 20cm (8 in) quiche tin. Bake
blind in the preheated oven for approximately 20 minutes.

4   Whisk the milk, cream, egg yolks, and thyme together. Layer the quiche case with the
fish and diced potato, season with black pepper. Pour the milk mixture over the top.
Return to the oven and cook for a further 35-40 minutes, until lightly browned on top
and set.

Fricassee of Seafood with Tomato Broth

(from Argyll)

Based on a classic French *bouillabaisse*, this is a stew for which you can use whatever fish you have available. I used to go down the pier at Tarbert on the Kintyre peninsula and watch the fishermen landing their catch. Every so often there would be an extra box in which they had tossed the odds and ends – perhaps a lone monkfish, or some small haddocks, plus a few prawns and small crabs. I could pick these up for next to nothing and assemble the basis of a feast. Once you've got the raw materials back to the kitchen, just imagine you are on a yacht off some west coast island and open a bottle or two of something dry and white!

Serves 4
Preparation time: 2 hours

2 tbsp olive oil
1 large onion, peeled and roughly chopped
1 leek, roughly chopped
1 carrot, peeled and roughly chopped
450g (1lb) ripe tomatoes
1 tsp tomato paste
2 cloves garlic, crushed
pinch of saffron

1.5 kg (3lb 4oz) fish bones
parsley stalks, bay leaf, fennel fronds
225ml (8fl oz/1 cup) white wine
salt and freshly ground black pepper
900g (2lb) of mixed fish, including monkfish or
    salmon, mussels in their shells, scallops and
    large prawn tails
chopped fresh parsley, to serve

1 Heat the olive oil in a large pan and sweat the onion, leek, and carrot until soft. Add the tomatoes, tomato paste, garlic and saffron and cook for 5 minutes. Add the fish bones and herbs. Add the wine and enough water to cover, and cook for 30 minutes. Strain the soup into a large clean pan, pressing the juices through the strainer.

2 Cut the fish in 5cm (2 in) pieces, scrub and debeard any mussels, and discard any that do not close when sharply tapped.

3 Return the soup to the heat and bring to a gentle simmer; check for seasoning and texture. If it is too thin then let it simmer for a while. If you like, add a splash of whisky or Pernod, which adds bite! The fish takes minutes to cook so add the firmer, larger

pieces first, such as monkfish or salmon, and mussels in their shells, and end with delicate scallops or prawn tails. Do not allow the soup to boil once you add the fish. Discard any mussels that do not open when cooked.

4 Scoop out the fish with a slotted spoon and distribute among 4 large soup plates and then ladle the broth over, and sprinkle liberally with parsley.

HAM AND HADDIE

(from Aberdeen)

The following recipe is delicious served cold as a lunch or supper dish or as a first course; it keeps very well covered in the fridge. Such a simple idea, but the two flavours really do create something different!

Serves 4
Preparation time: 30 mins

25g (1oz/2 tbsp) butter
4 fillets pale smoked haddock
4 slices ham (grilled/broiled bacon makes a
    perfectly good substitute)

115ml (4fl oz/^{1}/$_2$ cup) double (heavy) cream
freshly ground black pepper

1 Preheat the grill (broiler).

2 In a pan melt the butter and gently cook the haddock fillets, remove them to a heatproof dish and keep them warm; do not let them dry out.

3 Add the ham to the pan with the butter just to heat through, then place the ham on top of the haddock. Pour any haddock juices back into the pan, add the cream and simmer gently, seasoning with black pepper. Pour the cream mixture over the ham and haddock and place briefly under a hot grill (broiler). Serve immediately.

HIGHLANDS

The romantic Highlands, the last great wilderness in Britain, were largely a creation of the Victorians, with their sporting estates, hunting lodges, Landseer landscapes and admiration for the novels of Sir Walter Scott. The truth was somewhat grimmer: much of the wilderness was the result of the brutal Clearances, during which the landlords, many of them Scottish lairds, evicted their tenants to make more room for sheep. The tenants had been crofters, subsistence farmers, and fishermen, who had eked out a living in this hostile landscape for centuries, living on the sparse crops they could grow in the small stony fields and what they could harvest from the wild – though there are records of goats, chickens and even pigs being kept as far north as Wick. In-the-pot cookery must have been the norm here, with bread, such as bere bannocks (see page 117), being made from the native grains of the region.

Today, the farmers that remain survive only by courtesy of hill-farming subsidies, but the Highlands still offer a wonderful range of food, most of it harvested from the wild. The stocks of migratory salmon and sea trout may be sadly depleted, thanks, many argue, to the proliferation of salmon farms in the sea lochs of the west coast, but even if you avoid the mass-produced farmed salmon and stick to that reared under organic regimes, this is still a luxury product available at an astonishingly modest cost. And, for those prepared to seek them out, there are still gloriously golden-brown trout to be caught in the hill lochs, there are grouse and venison, mackerel, herrings, langoustine and lobsters, scallops and mussels, blueberries, even dulse, the edible seaweed harvested from the coastal beds. This last is eaten by the local sheep, especially the black-face breed from the islands, and gives their meat a remarkable flavour. And there is also, of course, the whisky to wash it all down with.

On the west coast, thanks to the Gulf Stream, the climate is astonishingly mild, and this coupled with the copious rainfall means that where fertile land can be found, vegetables will flourish. Testament to this is provided by the famous garden established at Inverewe by Osgood Mackenzie and now owned by The National Trust for Scotland; the kitchen garden there, on a terrace just above the shores of Loch Ewe (see page 6), must be one of the most beautiful vegetable plots in the world. You can enjoy it all the more in the knowledge that Mackenzie was one of the few lairds who did not 'clear' his land of people.

*Scallops and langoustines are just two expamples of the wealth of seafood
to be found in the sea lochs of the North West Highlands*

HERRING WITH RHUBARB RELISH

(from Argyll)

Herrings have been fished from Loch Fyne for centuries and have been kippered there for many years as well. Many of them were landed at Inveraray a town specially built to serve the fishing industry, though the town is now better known as a destination for tourists drawn by its Georgian frontage and, of course, its famous castle.

Serves 4
Preparation time: 45 mins

4 stalks rhubarb
50g (2 oz/4 tbsp) brown sugar
2 tsp wholegrain mustard

4 whole fresh herring, cleaned
salt and freshly ground black pepper
4 tbsp olive oil

1   Cut the rhubarb into 2.5cm (1in) pieces, wash and shake dry; place it in a pan with a well fitting lid, sprinkle the sugar over and add the wholegrain mustard. Stew gently over a low heat, with the lid on, for about 30 minutes, until the rhubarb is completely soft. Stir to combine well, set aside, and keep warm.

2   Preheat the grill (broiler) for at least 5 minutes. Line the grill (broiler) pan with foil.

3   Using a sharp knife, slash the fish 2 or 3 times down each side, season and brush with olive oil. Place in the grill (broiler) pan and grill (broil) each side for about 4 minutes until cooked. The slashes should open up to speed cooking and the skin should be lightly browned. Serve immediately with the rhubarb relish.

KEDGEREE

(from Aberdeen)

Where did this very popular dish originate? It is referred to in various old
recipe books, not least the Malcolm ones dating from 1790. I have always felt
that it must have been devised in the cookhouse of some Scottish regiment in
an effort to recreate the flavours of India. The old recipes used any sort of
white fish with cayenne pepper to spice things up; today, most recipes call for
smoked haddock and curry powder. Kedgeree is good for breakfast with,
perhaps, a blob of natural yoghurt.

Serves 4
Preparation time: 1 hour

25g (1oz/2 tbsp) butter
1 onion, peeled and finely chopped
350g (12oz/2 cups) long grain rice
750ml (27fl oz/3¹/₃ cups) chicken stock
bay leaf

4 fillets of undyed smoked haddock
a little milk
5 just hard-boiled eggs
2 tsp mild curry powder

1   Preheat the oven to 200°C (400°F/Gas 6).

2   In a large casserole with a lid, melt the butter and sweat the onion in it. Add the rice and
    turn until coated in the butter. Add the stock, and bring to the boil. Add the bay leaf.
    Cover and cook in the oven for 20 minutes.

3   Meanwhile, poach the fish in a little milk. When the rice is ready, remove from the
    oven: all the liquid should be absorbed. Roughly chop the eggs into the rice and flake in
    the fish too. Add the curry powder and mix in with a fork so as not to damage the rice.
    Season as required and serve hot.

FISH CAKES

(from Aberdeen)

Another idea based on Alison Mitchell's cooking at Crathes Castle. Basically,
this is my own recipe for fish cakes; in this instance I have used only smoked
haddock, but I have added the spring onions at Alison's suggestion. The best
potatoes for fishcakes are floury varieties such as King Edward or Golden
Wonder. Cook them in salted water and then drain them well, allowing as
much moisture to run off as possible, then return them to the pan and leave
on the heat for a while to really dry out.
The fish should be poached in milk with some seasoning such as a bay leaf,
thyme and a few peppercorns.

Serves 4
Preparation time: 1 hour 30 mins + cooling time

700g (1lb 8oz) smoked haddock
700g (1lb 8oz) dry, cooked mashed potato
salt and freshly ground black pepper
2 tsp chopped spring onions (scallions)
1 tbsp chopped fresh herbs such as parsley,
   chives, tarragon, chervil

seasoned plain (all-purpose) flour, for coating
2 eggs whisked with a little milk, for coating
fine, dry breadcrumbs, for coating
a little oil and 1 tsp butter, for shallow frying

1   Mix the fish together with the mashed potato, either in a food processor or by hand, but
keep a little texture in the mixture. Season with salt and pepper and add the spring
onions (scallions) and herbs.

2   Mould the fish mixture to make about 8 patties and chill for a few hours.

3   Arrange the coating ingredients in 3 separate dishes. Dip each patty into the seasoned
flour to coat thoroughly, then the whisked egg mixture, and finally the breadcrumbs,
again to coat well. If you like, repeat the egg and breadcrumb layers to make a thicker
coating.

4   Preheat the oven to 180°C (350°F/Gas 4). Heat the oil and butter in a frying pan and
cook the fish cakes until browned on each side, then place in the oven to heat through.
Serve with tartare sauce (see page 153).

Hew Lorimer's Abroath Smokies and Parsnips

(from Fife)

Smokies are small smoked haddock produced in the following manner: the fresh fish are gutted and the head removed before being dry-salted for about two hours; the fish are then tied in pairs and hung over wooden rods; the salt is washed off and the fish is left to dry for about five hours to toughen the skin before being put over the smoke pit and hot-smoked for just under an hour. Traditionally, they were prepared this way in the little village of Auchmithie, just north of Arbroath on the east coast, but at the start of the twentieth century the fishing folk moved to Arbroath, which is where smokies are still produced today. The Spink family, who have been producing smokies for generations, have managed to get an EU appellation attached to the smokie, so that, just as 'Champagne' must come from the area around Rheims or 'Parmesan' cheese from the Parma area, now only smokies produced within a delineated area around Arbroath can be called 'Arbroath Smokies'.

Smokies are delicious if served then and there straight from the smoke house! But it is not every day you happen to be passing Arbroath. If you do get them fresh, then just split them open, remove the backbone and eat them as they are. Alternatively, you can split them open and dot the inside with butter, then close them up, wrap them in foil and warm through in the oven; the bone comes out more easily when it has been warmed.

I have left this recipe just as Monica Heyman sent it to me, as no measurements are crucial except that I advise an oven of 180°C/350°F/gas 5. The generous spirit of her father, Hew Lorimer, the last of his line to live at Kellie Castle, seems to me to come through, coupled with an obvious understanding of quality ingredients.

Serve with baked potatoes and steamed purple sprouting broccoli or ragged jack kale, dressed with good olive oil, sea salt and a little lemon juice.

Serves 4
Preparation time: 1 hour 30 mins

6 parsnips
4 large Arbroath smokies (haddock that is
    dried, salted, then smoked, see above)
butter
sea salt and freshly ground black pepper

juice 1/2 lemon
300ml (10fl oz/1 1/4 cups) double (heavy) cream
chopped fresh parsley

1   Boil the whole parsnips till just soft, then slice fairly thinly.

2   Infuse the smokies by placing in a heat-resistant bowl and covering with boiling water for about 15 minutes. Drain and, when cool enough to handle, remove the skin and all bones.

3   Preheat the oven to 180°C/350°F/Gas 4.

4   Generously butter a large shallow baking dish and line with half the parsnip slices, scatter some shavings of butter over, and season with a little salt and pepper. Then layer on all of the smokies, seasoning with pepper only.

5   Place the remaining sliced parsnips on top, adding butter and seasoning as before; sprinkle over the lemon juice, then pour the cream over the whole dish.

6   Place in the oven for 25–30 minutes, until lightly brown on top. Scatter plenty of chopped fresh parsley over the dish before serving.

KIPPERS

(from Aberdeen)

Kippers have long been a staple and are usually associated with the west coast and Loch Fyne – there was a time when the number of kippers being sold as 'Loch Fyne' far exceeded the number of herrings actually caught in the loch! But nowadays kippers from all over Scotland are available. Kippers are in fact herrings split open, hung in pairs by the tail and smoked. If you are concerned about the smell during and after cooking, which puts a lot of people off, then follow this method, which will allow you to cook a kipper without stinking the house out.

Serves 1
Preparation time: 30 mins

1 kipper   butter

1   Preheat the oven to 190°C (375°F/Gas 5).

2   Butter a sheet of foil and place the kipper on top. Put a few more dots of butter on the fish and fold the foil over to make a parcel.

3   Place on a baking tray and bake in the oven for about 15 minutes, then serve the fish as it is, in the foil. The fortunate recipient can unwrap the fish themselves and eat it from the foil – when finished, the bones can be wrapped up and put straight into the bin! No dirty plates even!

FILLET OF HALIBUT WITH TURMERIC, MUSSELS AND HERB RISOTTO

(from Highlands)

This is where you can play around with combining different ideas in this book. I have taken halibut, a white fish, and combined it with mussels, as they go well together, and added a version of the risotto on page 107. In this case I suggest you don't use the leek and bacon in the risotto, but instead add 2 tablespoons of chopped mixed fresh herbs such as parsley, tarragon, chervil and coriander, but they must be fresh; dried herbs are an abomination which should only be used in dire emergencies and then only for casseroles which are to be cooked for at least 3 hours. Otherwise the risotto method is the same.

Serves 4
Preparation time: 45 mins

risotto (see below)
2 tbsp chopped mixed fresh herbs such as
   parsley, tarragon, chervil, and coriander
   (cilantro)
50g (2oz/¼ cup) butter
4 fillets halibut, about 175g (6oz) each

salt and freshly ground black pepper
¼ tsp turmeric
4 tbsp white wine
20 fresh mussels, scrubbed and beards removed
150ml (5fl oz/⅔ cup) double (heavy) cream
fresh herbs, to garnish

1   First make the risotto, following the recipe for Leek and Smoked Bacon Risotto, page 107. Omit the leek and bacon, and add the fresh herbs. Keep the risotto warm.

2   Heat a pan and melt the butter. Dry and season the halibut steaks. As the butter begins to bubble slightly, place them in the pan and cook on one side for about 1 minute. Turn them over, lower the heat slightly, and cook for about another 5 minutes until just cooked.

3   Remove the fish from the pan and keep it warm. Stir the turmeric into the pan, then add the wine and the mussels and cover. Steam gently until the mussels open. Discard any that do not open. Add the cream and allow to bubble gently, season and remove from the heat. You can serve the mussels in their shells or remove them from the shells, whichever you prefer.

4   Place a portion of risotto in the middle of each serving plate and put a halibut steak on top. Arrange the mussels around each serving. Check the sauce – if it is too thick, dilute it with a little water, or lemon juice if it needs sharpening. Spoon the sauce over the mussels. Garnish with fresh herbs and serve with steamed vegetables such as peas or beans if you like.

Red Fish with Tomatoes, Capers and Mustard Relish

(from Argyll)

This is such an easy recipe but calls for a little awareness! Red fish, or Norwegian haddock, is available over most Scottish fish counters, so ask your fishmonger for it and stop using haddock since we are slowly depleting our stocks. Mustard relish is made with whole grain mustard and is quite mild. There is a good brand made by Isabella Massie in Aberdeenshire which is available in many delis around Scotland.

Serves 4
Preparation time: 45 mins

4 fillets red fish (Norwegian haddock)
a little oil and butter
6 tomatoes, skinned, seeded, and diced
2 tsp mustard relish
chopped fresh herbs, such as marjoram,
  oregano, fennel fronds

2 tsp capers, roughly chopped
white wine
salt and freshly ground black pepper

1   Dry the fish well and heat the oil in a heavy-based pan. Add the butter and cook the fish until lightly brown, turn over and complete cooking. Remove from the pan and keep warm.

2   Quickly add the tomatoes to the pan and stir to heat through. Add the mustard relish, fresh herbs and capers and mix gently. Add a splash of white wine and season to taste.

3   Serve the tomato mixture with the fish fillets arranged on top.

Oysters

(from Argyll)

I cannot write about Scottish seafood, especially when I think of Argyll, without at least a mention of oysters! Since my first introduction to them as a child I have gone on to enjoy these wonderful shellfish more and more, and it has to be said the best do come from Scotland!

There is something about the rich smooth creamy texture with that faintly briney finish which is entirely satisfying. If you have never tried them before, start by eating them with nothing on – I don't mean that you should have no clothes on (although as they are supposed to be an aphrodisiac, that may be a good idea). No, I mean that, once opened, try them just like that. Don't swallow the oyster whole but savour the texture and have a chew, then swallow; there is a lovely rich creamy after-taste which goes so well with Guinness! For variation try them topped with finely chopped shallots moistened with a little red wine vinegar, or a spoon of honey on each oyster followed by some chopped spring onions and a splash of soy sauce. Then put them under a hot grill for four minutes. However you eat them always make sure they are fresh and Scottish – delicious!

WHOLE SALMON TO SERVE COLD

(from Argyll)

I once read of a recipe developed by the great Robert Carrier in which he cooked a whole salmon in a dishwashing machine! A great idea as many people don't have an oven big enough to hold a whole fish. Do try it, but don't blame me if it doesn't work. And don't put any soap in!
Here is a more traditional method.

Serves 8
Preparation time: 1 hour 30 mins

1.5 kg (3¼ lb) salmon, cleaned and scaled
olive oil
salt and freshly ground black pepper

1 bay leaf
8–10 sprigs of thyme
8–10 fresh parsley stalks

1 Preheat the oven to 160°C (325°F/Gas 3).

2 It is best if you cook the fish whole but if it is too big then cut off the head and/or tail. Take a piece of foil large enough to wrap the fish and use about 2 teaspoons olive oil to cover the foil where the fish will sit. Rinse and dry the fish well, then rub the fish with olive oil and seasoning and stuff the cavity with herbs.

3 Wrap up the fish quite loosely in the foil and bake in the oven for 1 hour. (To check if it is cooked, it should feel firm when pushed gently; if it is slightly springy, then it isn't.) Either allow the salmon to cool quickly and refrigerate, or serve warm with a Hollandaise sauce.

ARGYLL

One of my most favourite regions of Scotland. I have lived and worked in Argyll and it was often the holiday destination of my youth. This was the area I first came to when I returned to work in Scotland and, along with my wife Caroline, ran the Portsonachan Hotel on Loch Awe. The return was a revelation: I discovered so many new ingredients, not just the fish and game but wild herbs, mushrooms and berries. Argyll is full of this kind of 'wild' food.

One of my chef heroes has always been Roger Verge from France and I remember one of his recipes was for rabbit 'on its favourite bed'. In other words, he used ingredients from the environment of the animal in question. In Argyll this is a theme on which it is possible to play many variations: venison flavoured with blueberries, grouse with heather, fish steamed with seaweed, whatever the time of year there is always something to cook and something to cook it with!

The quality of the shellfish is fantastic; Argyll has a coastline longer than that of France and Spain put together, honeycombed with ins and outs, gulleys and coves, where the crashing Atlantic ocean creates an environment ideal for fish and shellfish. Much of it is farmed today, of course, from salmon to mussels and, more recently, cod and sea bass. If we are going to go on enjoying the fruits of the sea then this is the only way in which we are going to be able to keep up a supply. Happily, increasing environmental concern has made many sea-farmers more aware of the importance of looking after this great natural resource, and recently we have seen more organic produce as well as stricter control over methods of production.

My childhood holidays were mainly spent on the island of Iona, where we had a cottage. We would trawl for fish in the sea, gutting and cleaning them and taking them to my mum to grill for supper. It was here that I was introduced by her to bog myrtle, which she would pick on a walk and use to enhance the flavour of a lamb stew.

Scottish rope-grown mussels – real fast food which takes just minutes to prepare and seconds to cook.

Spiced Herring

(from Argyll)

The quick cooking of the fish combines with the freshness of the marinade to make a lovely dish. This is especially good as a first course or a lunch dish; the fish are also delicious served cold with a potato salad.

Serves 4
Preparation time: 1 hour 30 mins + marinading time

4 herring, filleted and boned
2 tbsp olive oil

For the marinade:
150ml (5fl oz/²/₃ cup) olive oil
150ml (5fl oz/²/₃ cup) white
    wine vinegar
1 tbsp clear honey
1 clove garlic, crushed

2 tbsp fresh coriander, chopped
2 tbsp fresh parsley, chopped
1 tbsp fresh chives, chopped
1 tsp crushed coriander seeds

1   First make the marinade. Combine the oil and wine vinegar with the honey and whisk together; add the crushed garlic, the fresh herbs and coriander seeds. Leave to stand for about 1 hour.

2   Wipe the fish clean and then, using a sharp knife, make about 2 or 3 slashes down the skin side of each.

3   Heat a frying pan and add the olive oil. Fry the fish, skin side down, very quickly, until browned a little. The slashes will help to stop the fish from curling in the heat, help it cook quicker, and look good as the colour of the flesh shows through the skin. Turn the fish over and cook them on the other side; the whole process will take about 5 minutes.

4   Put the fish fillets on a serving dish, and while still hot pour the marinade over them and leave to cool for at least 6 hours before serving.

Trout Cooked with Gooseberries

(from Argyll)

Brown trout are the principal indigenous fish in many Scottish lochs and rivers and a freshly caught and cooked one is delicious! Nowadays, with the onset of trout farming, it is the rainbows, originally imported from Canada, which are reared, as they grow a great deal faster than the browns. While perhaps not quite so good as their native counterparts, the rainbows do look pretty with their shimmering colouring – hence the name – and are very tasty cooked in this way.

Serves 4
Preparation time: 45 mins

250g (9oz/1 cup) gooseberries
25g (1oz/2 tbsp) brown sugar
4 trout, cleaned and splayed open
salt and freshly ground black pepper

150g (5oz/1 cup) medium oatmeal
1 tbsp vegetable oil
85g (3oz/¹/₃ cup) butter

1 First make the sauce: in a small pan cook the gooseberries very gently in a little water with the sugar. A purée will form which will have some texture and some pieces of fruit.

2 Meanwhile, season the trout and press the open belly down on to a board, pushing firmly down the backbone. Turn the trout over and remove the spine – it should come out quite easily.

3 Coat both sides of the fish with oatmeal. Heat a large pan with the oil and add the butter; place the trout in the pan, flesh side down, and cook on a high heat for 2 minutes until the oatmeal is lightly coloured. Reduce the heat and cook for a further 2 minutes.

4 Turn the trout over, and cook for 4 minutes at the lower heat, basting occasionally with the butter. Serve with the gooseberry sauce.

STEAMED MUSSELS
WITH COCONUT AND TURMERIC

(from Argyll)

Mussels are the most delicious of shellfish, and on the west coast they can often be collected wild off the rocks at low tide. Today, however, there are many mussel farms which grow them on ropes suspended in sea lochs. In this way they are washed by strong tides and feed naturally from the water. They need little cleaning since they don't get covered with the barnacles. I remember spending hours as a child cleaning the barnacles off the ones we gathered from the rocks!

Serves 4
Preparation time: 45 mins

about 1.35 kg (3lb) fresh mussels
50g (2oz/¼ cup) butter
1 onion, peeled and chopped
½ tsp turmeric
150ml (5fl oz/⅔ cup) dry white wine
bay leaf

sprig of thyme
6 peppercorns
150ml (5fl oz/⅔ cup) double (heavy) cream
1 tsp grated coconut cream
freshly ground black pepper
chopped fresh parsley

1   Scrub the mussels in plenty of cold water and discard any which remain open when tapped lightly. Remove the beards with a sharp knife.

2   Melt the butter in a heavy-based pan and sweat the onion gently until soft; add the turmeric and stir for a few minutes – this cooks out the acrid flavour turmeric can have.

3   Add the mussels with the wine, herbs and peppercorns. Cover and steam over a medium heat until the mussel shells open; this will take about 5 minutes. Discard any that do not open.

4   Remove the lid from the pan and add the cream and the coconut. Simmer rapidly to allow the sauce to thicken slightly. Remove the bay leaf and thyme sprig. Serve immediately in bowls with a grind or two of pepper and lots of chopped parsley and crusty bread. Heaven!

Tweed Kettle

(from Borders)

Here is a traditional recipe, but do not be afraid to use farmed salmon if you cannot get wild fish. Those produced in the Shetland Islands are excellent because they are not overcrowded and are allowed space to move about to develop their muscle structure; equally good is the salmon sold under the brand of Loch Fyne Oysters, this is farmed for the firm in the far north of Scotland under strong conservation ideals.

As the name suggests, this is a recipe which comes from the Borders area, where the famous salmon waters of the River Tweed flow. It is an old recipe and I particularly like the fact that it uses ingredients which would have been introduced into Scotland – mace from the eastern trade, wine imported from France through Leith – combined with the high-quality, locally sourced main ingredient.

Serves 4
Preparation time: 1 hour

1kg (2¼ lb) fresh salmon
salt and freshly ground black pepper
pinch of mace
150ml (5fl oz/⅔ cup) dry white wine
2 shallots, peeled and chopped

50g (2oz/¼ cup) butter
115g (4oz) mushrooms, chopped
2 tsp chopped fresh chives
1 tbsp chopped fresh parsley

1   Put the salmon in a pan in which it fits neatly, add water just to cover and poach the fish gently for about 5 minutes. Remove from the pan and reserve the cooking liquor.

2   When cool enough, remove all the skin and bones from the salmon, add them to the cooking liquor and simmer for 10 minutes. Strain and reserve the liquor.

3   Cut the fish into cubes about 5cm (2in) across. Season with salt, pepper and mace. Put into a clean pan with 150ml (5 fl oz/ ⅔ cup) of the fish liquor, the wine and shallots. Cover and gently simmer for about 10 minutes.

4   Meanwhile, heat the butter in a pan and stew the mushrooms gently for 2 or 3 minutes; add the chives, drain off the liquid, and add the mushrooms and chives to the salmon. Serve sprinkled with the chopped parsley and with mashed potatoes.

MEAT

BOBOTI

(from Fife)

Or 'Bobbity' as the Crichton Stuart family of Falkland Palace and Myres Castle used to call it. This is a recipe given to the family by a relative who lived in South Africa who knew General Smuts. It comes from the book *Quality Fare* and is inscribed 'Durban 1967'. I have updated the measurements.

Serves 4
Preparation time: 1 hour 30 mins

50g (2oz/¼ cup) butter, and extra for greasing
1 large onion, chopped
450g (1lb) raw minced (ground) beef or lamb
1 slice white bread soaked in 115ml
(4fl oz/½ cup) milk
25g (1oz/¼ cup) ground almonds

50g (2oz/⅓ cup) raisins
salt and freshly ground black pepper
1 tbsp curry powder
juice of 1 lemon
4 lemon leaves
2 eggs, beaten

1   Preheat oven to 180°C (350°F/Gas 4).

2   Melt the butter in a frying pan and add the chopped onion; fry until softened. Add the meat and fry until lightly coloured.

3   Add the soaked bread, ground almonds, raisins, salt, pepper, and curry powder. Cook for about 5 minutes, stirring to prevent sticking.

4   Transfer to a buttered pie dish and bake in the oven for 30 minutes. Remove from the oven, sprinkle over the lemon juice, and push the lemon leaves into the mixture. Cover with the beaten eggs, return to the oven and cook until set – about 10 minutes.

5   Serve with rice and chutney; it is also good cold with a salad.

BRAISED LAMB SHANKS WITH PUY LENTILS

(from Highlands)

Lamb shanks are one of my favourite cuts of meat. Long, slow cooking brings
out the richness of flavour and texture, while the addition of the smoked
venison adds a lovely edge.

Serves 4
Preparation time: 4 hours

4 lamb shanks, total weight about 2kg (4lb 8oz)
salt and freshly ground black pepper
2 tbsp olive oil
1 large onion, peeled and diced
1 large carrot, peeled and diced
1 large leek, peeled and diced

450g (1lb) Puy lentils
3 cloves garlic, crushed with salt
350g (12oz) can chopped tomatoes
1 tbsp tomato purée
1 bay leaf
6 slices smoked venison, cut into strips

1 Preheat the oven to 230°C (450°F/Gas 8).

2 Season the lamb shanks, place them in a large deep casserole, and smother them in the
   olive oil. Roast in the oven for about 10 minutes until well coloured. Turn the oven down
   to 190°C (375°F/Gas 5) and continue to cook for about 1 hour 30 minutes.

3 Remove the casserole from the oven and add the diced vegetables; stir them into the
   juices and return to the oven for about 30 minutes.

4 Meanwhile, rinse the lentils in cold water and put in a pan, and cover with cold water;
   bring to the boil and simmer for about 15 minutes then drain well.

5 When the lamb is cooked, transfer the casserole to the stove top. Remove the lamb
   shanks and set them aside. Add the garlic to the casserole and stir in, then add the
   lentils and the tomatoes, tomato purée and bay leaf. Simmer for about 10 minutes until
   the lentils are soft but still holding their shape.

6 Stir in the strips of smoked venison. Return the shanks to the casserole and cover with
   the lentil mixture. Cook for another 30 minutes in the oven. The lamb should be falling
   off the bone and the lentils soft with a little bite to them. Remove the bay leaf before
   serving.

Braised Shoulder of Lamb with Dulse

(from Highlands

Dulse is a seaweed, or sea vegetable as the purists will call it, and has been part of the Highland way of life for centuries; it is now available from specialist food outlets in Scotland and beyond. It has excellent properties for all sorts of things. Sheep on the islands eat it, adding a briney flavour to their meat. Farmers collect it off the beach to spread on the land as fertilizer, and it is still used today in soaps and the confectionery industry because of its gelatinous properties. Dulse has a strong flavour and is good in stews and soups; once dried it can simply be crumbled into soups as a flavour enhancer. Do not pick the dead stuff off the beach; like any vegetable, dulse needs to be harvested from growing plants, usually out to sea. At low tides it is possible to collect it, but it is better to buy the dried variety from health shops.

Serves 8
Preparation time: 4 hours

1 shoulder of lamb, boned and rolled, about
   1.8kg (4lb)
2 tbsp olive oil
15g ($^1/_2$ oz/1 tbsp) butter

3 onions, peeled and sliced
50g (2oz) dried dulse (sea vegetable)
1 litre (35fl oz/4$^1/_2$ cups) water
salt and freshly ground black pepper

1   Use a deep casserole into which the lamb will fit, with a lid. Dry the lamb and heat the olive oil in the casserole. Brown the lamb all over in the oil, turning it over on all sides; this will take about 10 minutes. Take the lamb out and remove any excess fat from the casserole.

3   Add the butter to the casserole, add the onions and cook until well browned and then place the lamb back on top. Sprinkle in the dulse, pour on the water, and add 5 grinds of a pepper mill (no salt at this stage).

3   Bring to the boil and simmer, covered, very gently on the stove top for about 2 hours Alternatively, cook in a preheated oven at 180°C (350°F/Gas 4) for about 2 hours.

4   When the lamb is cooked, remove from the casserole and turn the heat up to reduce the liquid down to about 200ml (7fl oz/scant 1 cup). Strain the reduced liquid, pushing the onions through the sieve with the back of a ladle or spoon. Check the sauce for seasoning and serve, slicing the lamb in thick slices and coating with the sauce.

CLAPSHOT COTTAGE PIE

(from Glasgow)

This dish is a contemporary take on good, old-fashioned cottage pie, a real comfort food which can only have originated in a British kitchen. The addition of a traditional Orcadian dish (clapshot) as a topping is, in my opinion, simply brilliant, even if it is only a slight move away from the original, and I unashamedly borrow one of Sue Lawrence's ideas.

Serves 4
Preparation time: 2 hours

1 tbsp vegetable oil
1 onion, peeled and chopped
450g (1lb) minced (ground) beef or minced (ground) cooked beef from a roast
2 tsp plain (all-purpose) flour
150ml (5fl oz/²/₃ cup) beef stock
1 tbsp tomato purée
1 tbsp Worcestershire sauce

salt and freshly ground black pepper
1 tbsp chopped fresh parsley
400g (14oz) potatoes, peeled and chopped
400g (14oz) turnip (rutabaga), peeled and chopped
40g (1¹/₂ oz/3 tbsp) butter
1 tbsp chopped fresh chives

1   Heat the oil in a heavy-based pan, sweat the onion gently for about 10 minutes, then increase the heat and add the minced beef. Brown the meat all over, using a wooden spoon to break it up.

2   Add the flour and stir in, then the hot stock. Bring to the boil, adding the purée and Worcestershire sauce. Season and add the parsley. Cook for about 15 minutes. Pour into an ovenproof dish.

3   Preheat the oven to 180°C (350°F/Gas 4).

4   In a pan of boiling water, cook the potatoes and turnips together until tender, then drain well. Mash with the butter, season, and add the chives. Spread over the meat and bake in the oven for 40 minutes until hot through and lightly browned.

FORFAR BRIDIES

(from Aberdeen)

Makes 10 'pasties' (turnovers)
Preparation time: 2 hours

1.25kg (2³/₄lb) rump steak (topside),
    cut into 1cm (¹/₂ in) slices
225g (8oz) beef suet, finely chopped
5 onions, peeled and finely chopped
salt and freshly ground black pepper
butter, for greasing

For the pastry:
225g (8oz/1 cup) butter
225g (8oz/1 cup) lard (shortening)
900g (2lb/8 cups) plain (all-purpose) flour, plus
    extra for dusting
salt

1   Preheat the oven to 200°C (400°F/Gas 6).

2   To make the pastry, rub the fat into the flour until you have the consistency of breadcrumbs, add the salt, and mix with water until you have a very stiff dough. Divide into 10 equal-sized pieces and roll out on a floured board to give 10 large ovals.

3   Trim off any fat from the steak and cut roughly into 1cm (¹/₂ in) squares. Put the meat into a bowl with the suet and onions. Add seasoning and mix well.

4   Divide the meat mixture into 10 portions and cover half of each oval with meat, leaving a rim for sealing. Wet the edges of the dough, fold over and seal, using your finger and thumb to crimp the edge. Pierce a hole in the top of each pastie with a skewer. Bake the pasties on greased baking sheets for 45 minutes until golden brown and cooked through. Serve warm.

HAGGIS

(from Glasgow)

No book on Scottish cooking would be complete without some reference to haggis. Most people nowadays will prefer to buy their haggis ready-made, in which case I find the best way to reheat it is to wrap it in foil and bake in a preheated oven at 180°C (350°F/Gas 4). A 450g (1lb) haggis will take about 1 hour. Serve with mashed 'tatties' (potatoes) and bashed (mashed) 'neeps' (turnips/rutabaga).

But if you want to make your own you should be warned that this is not a recipe for the faint-hearted. Proper haggis is not normally made outside a butcher's shop or factory nowadays because the process is involved, not all the ingredients are available over the counter and it is really only worth making in bulk! I got this recipe from my butcher, Bob Kirkcaldy in Lundin Links, who holds it in his head and showed me how to make it. The word Bob uses for the broth is 'bray', which is interesting as the word 'bree' is the old word for a stock or soup, as in 'Partan Bree' crab soup. The pronunciation must be the Fife way.

mixture of sheep or lamb lites (lungs), hearts, and liver (half the quantity should be lites and then ¼ quantity each hearts and liver)
a similar quantity of fresh suet
2 onions
the above ingredients should weigh about 3kg (7lb)

oatmeal, coarse and fine
salt and freshly ground black pepper
ground cloves
haggis bung or skin
    (the intestine from a lamb or sheep)

1   Place the lites in a large pan (they increase in size during cooking), cover in water, and simmer over a low heat.

2   Trim the cartilage and any fat from the hearts and cut up, then trim the liver and cut up. Add to the lites after 1 hour and cook for another 2 hours.

3   Allow to cool, then remove the meat from the 'bray' (stock) and mince (grind) with the suet and onions.

4   Weigh the resulting mix. For every 4.5kg (10lb) of mix add 1.35kg (3lb) of oatmeal, in quantities 2 parts coarse:1 part fine.

5   Mix well, then weigh again. For every 6kg (13lb) of mix add 15g (½ oz) of seasoning and ½ tsp cloves. Mix together adding a little of the 'bray' to get the correct texture. It should be moist but not too heavy.

6   Stuff into skins to the size of your choice, and tie with kitchen string. To cook, place in a pan of cold water and bring to the boil. Boil for 1½ hours, and leave to cool in the water.

STRIPS OF BEEF RUMP WITH CHANTERELLES

(from Aberdeen)

The trick here is to use really good beef with no fat and to zap the dried pieces
quickly so that the outside is well browned and the inside very rare; so,
depending on how brave you are with the heat, cut the pieces either larger
(not brave) or smaller (brave). Serve with a pilaf rice (see kedgeree, page 49).

Serves 2
Preparation time: 30 mins

3 tbsp olive oil

2 rump steaks (about 175g (6oz) each), cut into
    strips

1 shallot, peeled and finely chopped

1 clove garlic, crushed

115g (4oz) chanterelles

salt and freshly ground black pepper

4 tbsp white wine

4 tbsp double (heavy) cream

25g (1oz/2 tbsp) butter

1 tbsp chopped fresh parsley

pilaf rice, to serve (optional)

1   Heat 2 tablespoons of the olive oil in a large frying pan. Dry the meat thoroughly so
that it cooks quickly. Place the meat in the pan and quickly colour the strips on both
sides. Do not put too many in at a time; it is better to fry in batches or the meat may
poach rather than fry. Remove the meat and set aside, keeping it warm.

2   Add the remaining olive oil to the frying pan and lower the heat. Stir in the shallot and
garlic, stir for about 1 minute.

3   Increase the heat and add the mushrooms, season and cook until they just start to
soften. Add the wine, bring to the boil and add the cream. As the liquid thickens, return
the beef to the pan and heat through.

4   Remove from the heat and swirl in the butter. Serve on warm plates, sprinkled with
chopped parsley, and with pilaf rice, if you like. (For the pilaf rice, follow steps 1 and 2
of the Kedgeree recipe, see page 49.)

OSSO BUCCO FLORENTINE

(from Edinburgh)

Another foreign influence here, but one which carries a real stigma. I remember
when veal was produced in a pretty unpleasant manner. Young male calves, a by-
product of the dairy industry, were put into small crates so they couldn't move, to
keep their flesh tender, and were kept in a dark shed, to keep the meat white; but
although the result was beautiful white, tender meat it had no flavour. Happily,
the crating of calves is now banned in the UK, but we still have the problem of
what to do with the male calves born to dairy herds. There are a number of farms
making an attempt to produce veal in an humane way, giving the animals some life
and making better use of them than just slaughtering them at birth. It is lovely
meat and worth looking for. There is a butcher on Islay, Gilbert MacTaggart,who
is trying to market the meat. I include a classic Italian recipe here simply because
osso bucco is a superb way of preparing a delicious meat. So throw away your
preconceived prejudices and try this!

Serves 4
Preparation time: 3 hours

1 veal shank, cut into 4 x 5cm (2 in) slices
  (including the bone)
50g (2oz/¹⁄₂ cup) plain (all-purpose) flour,
  seasoned with salt and pepper for coating
5 tbsp olive oil
2 small onions, peeled and chopped
2 stalks celery, diced
2 small carrots, diced
1 tsp crushed garlic
2 bay leaves

salt
350ml (12fl oz/1 ¹⁄₂ cups) white wine
2 tsp grated lemon zest
175ml (6fl oz/³⁄₄ cup) veal or chicken stock
800g (28oz) can plum tomatoes
1 tsp chopped fresh thyme
1 tsp chopped fresh rosemary
1 tbsp chopped fresh parsley

1   Preheat the oven to 180°C (350°F/Gas 4).

2   Coat the pieces of meat in the flour. Heat half the olive oil in a heavy-based casserole
    large enough to hold the shanks in one layer and that has a good lid. Brown the pieces
    on all sides, about 3 minutes. Remove and set aside.

3   Add the remaining oil and then add the onions, celery and carrots, brown gently but
    make sure they don't burn. Add half the garlic, the bay leaves, and some salt, stir in,

then add the wine and 1 tsp of the lemon zest. Stir to scrape up the juices, and allow to reduce by about half.

4   Add the stock, tomatoes, thyme and rosemary, and stir together. Return the meat to the pan. The contents should about ³/₄ fill the casserole, if not add some water.

5   Cover and cook in the oven for about 2 hours, turning the shanks 3 or 4 times during cooking, and adding water if it seems to be getting dry. When cooked, the meat should be coming away from the bone.

6   Remove the pieces and place on a serving platter. Reduce the sauce until it is of a coating consistency. Remove the bay leaves and pour the sauce over the meat.

7   Make a 'gremolata': mix together the remaining lemon zest, garlic, and the parsley and sprinkle over the top before serving.

COLLOPS IN THE PAN

(from Aberdeen)

Serves 4
Preparation time: 45 mins

85g (3oz/¹/₃ cup) butter
1 tbsp vegetable oil
4 onions, peeled and sliced
8 collops of beef (0.5cm/¹/₄ in thick slices fillet
  steak)

1 tbsp pickled walnut juice; if you cannot get
  pickled walnuts, use mushroom ketchup (see
  page 153)
salt and freshly ground black pepper

1   Heat half the butter with the oil in a heavy-based pan, brown the onions over a high heat, and turn them constantly with a wooden spoon. Reduce the heat and cook for 10 more minutes to soften. Remove the onions from the pan and keep warm.

2   Wipe the pan out, add the remaining butter, and return to the heat. Wipe the collops dry with kitchen paper (paper towels), and when the butter is foaming put the collops in and colour them on both sides - about 4 minutes. Remove them from the pan.

3   Return the onions to the pan, heat through, and add the walnut juice. Season with salt and pepper. To serve, arrange the onions in a mound on a serving dish with the steaks on top.

PORK FILLET WITH AVOCADO AND SAGE

(from Edinburgh)

This is such a simple idea, Italian I believe, and so good!

Serves 4
Preparation time: 30 mins

3 pork fillets about 400g (14oz) each, trimmed
1 avocado
50g (2oz/4 tbsp) butter

salt and freshly ground black pepper
2 tsp roughly chopped fresh sage leaves
juice of ½ lemon

1   Cut the pork fillets into 4 across the grain and flatten them with the side of a large knife between 2 sheets of cling film (plastic wrap).

2   Cut the avocado in half, prise apart and remove the stone and peel; place cut side down and slice both sides thinly, set aside. (If you do this in advance, squeeze some lemon juice over them to prevent discolouring.)

3   In a large frying pan, melt half the butter; dry the pieces of pork and season with salt and pepper. As the butter fizzles, place the meat carefully in the pan and colour quickly over high heat, turning to brown all over; reduce the heat and fry until cooked through – about 5 minutes. If necessary, fry the pork in batches.

4   Remove the pork pieces from the pan and place on 4 heated plates; arrange the avocado slices on top. Sprinkle the sage over the pork and avocado.

5   Add the remaining butter to the pan and stir to collect the juices. When the butter begins to darken slightly, add the lemon juice. When the bubbling has died down, spoon the liquid over the pork pieces. Serve with mashed potatoes and spring greens, if you like.

RAGOUT OF PORK WITH LEEKS AND PRUNES

(from Edinburgh)

I don't have many recipes for pork as it is not a very traditional thing in
Scotland, but I have included this one as it represents the foreign influences
which have become part of the Scottish tradition. The wine and prunes would
have come from France, but of course the leeks could be very local.

Serves 4
Preparation time: 45 mins + overnight soaking

8 prunes
300ml (10fl oz/1¼ cups) medium white wine
450g (1lb) pork fillet, trimmed
plain (all-purpose) flour, seasoned with salt and
    pepper, for coating

2 tbsp olive oil
1 tsp butter
225g (8oz) leeks, washed and sliced
300ml (10fl oz/1¼ cups) double (heavy) cream
1 tsp chopped fresh thyme

1   Soak the prunes overnight in the wine and then remove the stones.

2   Cut the pork into chunks and lightly coat in the seasoned flour. Heat a pan with the
olive oil and brown the pork all over; set aside.

3   Add the butter to the pan, reduce the heat, and add the leeks. Cook gently until they
are soft.

4   Add the prunes and wine, stirring up any bits from the pan base. Return the pork to the
pan and cook gently for about 5 minutes until the pork is cooked through (don't overdo
it or it will become tough).

5   When the pork is cooked, remove it from the pan and add the cream. Reduce the sauce
slightly until it just begins to thicken, then add the fresh thyme. Return the pork to the
pan to heat through and serve immediately.

FIFE

I am unashamedly partisan about this region; although I was born in Aberdeen, I now live in Fife and work at the wonderful 16th-century Myres Castle. Myres is just down the road from Falkland Palace, the country home of the Stuart kings and queens. Mary, Queen of Scots is said to have stayed at Myres and there is a tree in the grounds under which she sheltered from the rain while out riding from the Palace at Falkland. In those days, Fife, the playground of Scottish royalty, was covered in forest and deer and wild boar were hunted there.

When the King or Queen was in residence at Falkland the court was, no doubt, plentifully supplied with venison and boar from the surrounding forest. But woe betide those who fell into disfavour: they were traditionally banished to the nearby village of Freuchie with the words, 'Awa tae Freuchie and nae meat!' Even now, if the locals lose patience with you they are still likely to cut the conversation short with a curt, 'Och, awa tae Freuchie.'

Today most of the forest has been cleared and the deer and wild boar in Fife are farmed, but there are compensations in the form of the excellent fruit produced in the region, including much soft fruit such as strawberries, raspberries and Tayberries. There is still a strong fishing tradition in the pretty coastal villages of the East Neuk, like Pittenweem, St Monans and Anstruther, where first-class fish and shellfish are landed.

While researching this book I approached people who lived, or still live, in properties run by The National Trust for Scotland. One of the most helpful responses came from Elly Crichton Stuart, whose family have lived at Falkland Palace since it was purchased by her grandfather, the third Marquess of Bute, in 1887. Elly's brother, Ninian, is the current Captain, Keeper and Constable of Falkland (his father appointed The National Trust for Scotland as Deputy Keeper in 1952) and Baron of Myres.

Elly recalled a luncheon party she gave for her godfather, the sculptor Hew Lorimer (see his recipe for Arbroath smokies, page 52) and other friends for which, inspired by her mother's love of Italian food, she served pigeon breasts (see recipe page 91) followed by a 'Mont Blanc', a version of the zabaglione recipe included in this book (page 147).

From farmed deer to pheasant and wood pigeons,
Fife has it all.

SPICED BEEF

(from Glasgow)

Another old-fashioned way of preserving food is to use spices, and meats would often have been treated in this manner, which allows a whole animal to be preserved.

Serves 9
Preparation time: 9 days

3kg (6lb 8oz) piece of topside of beef
2 carrots, roughly chopped
2 small onions, peeled and roughly chopped
300ml (10fl oz/1 ¼ cups) water

For the spice mix:
115g (4oz/ ⅔ cup) dark brown sugar
115g (4oz/ ½ cup) sea salt
25g (1oz/2 tsp) black peppercorns
25g (1oz/2 tsp) white peppercorns
15g (½ oz) allspice
15g (½ oz) coriander seeds
25g (1oz) juniper berries

1   Trim off all the excess fat from the meat and rub the sugar into the meat all over. Leave for 2 days in a cool place.

2   Crush together all the other spice mix ingredients and rub this into the meat. Refrigerate. Turn the beef every day for about a week: the longer it's left the stronger the spice flavour will become.

3   When ready to cook the beef, preheat the oven to 150°C (300°F/Gas 2).

4   Rinse the spice mixture off the beef; put the carrots and onions in a large casserole and put the beef on top. Add the water. Cover tightly and cook for 4 hours in the oven, basting the meat with the liquid from time to time.

5   Remove the meat from the casserole and press firmly into a large loaf tin. Cover with cling film (plastic wrap), and weight the top. Allow to cool then put in the refrigerator until completely cold.

6   Serve cold – it is excellent with baked potatoes and pickles.

Spicy Lamb Stew with Apricots

(from Glasgow)

Another hybrid. Good lamb is a Scottish staple, but the use of apricots to sweeten it and the spices to give it a sort of curried flavour are unusual. This recipe comes from Mrs Young who ran the Portsonachan Hotel for many years. I am sure the idea for this will have come from her time in India, where her husband served in the army.

Serves 4
Preparation time: 2 hours

700g (1lb 8oz) meat from leg of lamb, diced
2 tbsp olive oil
450g (1lb) onions, peeled and sliced

½ tsp each ground ginger, nutmeg, cloves and curry powder
225g (8oz/2 cups) dried apricots

1   Dry the meat thoroughly with kitchen paper (paper towels). Heat the olive oil in a large frying pan, and brown the pieces of meat in the pan, taking care not to put too many in at once. Using a slotted spoon, transfer the meat to a casserole.

2   Add the onions to the frying pan and fry until just browned; add them to the lamb. Add the spices to the casserole and top up with enough water to just cover the meat.

3   Simmer over a low heat for about 1 hour 15 minutes, then add the apricots and continue to simmer for another 15 minutes. Alternatively, you can cook it in a 180°C (350°F/Gas 4) oven. Like most stews this is best kept at least a day for the flavours to develop, and the apricots and onions provide a lovely texture.

STOVIES

(from Glasgow)

One of those classic Scottish dishes which makes use of left-overs to create an entirely new dish. There are many derivations of the basic recipe, some more successful than others. It seems to me that it could be made with any cold meat but probably lamb or beef are best. Beware the stovies made with tinned meat or mashed potato! They just do not get the texture created by the stock combining with the starch in the potatoes to produce a lovely rich gravy.

Serves 4
Preparation time: 2 hours 30 mins

1 tbsp dripping (meat drippings or lard)
1 large onion, peeled and sliced
115g (4oz) cold cooked lamb, diced

700g (1lb 8oz) potatoes, peeled and evenly sliced
salt and freshly ground black pepper
300ml (10fl oz/1 ¼ cups) beef stock

1   Preheat the oven to 190°C (375°F/Gas 5).

2   Melt the dripping in a large pan, add the onion and cook gently to soften and lightly brown.

3   In a casserole, layer first the sliced potatoes, then the meat, and lastly the onions, seasoning as you go. Add the stock to cover.

4   Cook in the oven for about 50 minutes, until the liquid is absorbed and the edges of the potatoes are browned.

To cook a Ham in comfort

(from Glasgow)

This is a wonderful recipe which came from a book belonging to my mother. Pork is comparatively little used in Scotland, where it is, to my mind, much underrated, especially as there are so many ways of preparing it, from delicious roasts – I always maintain that the best roast gravy comes from pork – to cures of all kinds. I buy my hams or gammon from Tom Mitchell in Auchtertool and although the pigs are bred conventionally, you do get a lovely flavour when you cook one of his joints in this way. Hams keep very well and are a great asset to have around at Christmas time for all those family gatherings; ham and baked potatoes make a delicious, almost instant, meal!

Serves 20 or more
Preparation time: 6 hours + 24 hours soaking

1 whole green (fresh unsmoked) ham	6 cloves
4 carrots, roughly chopped	bunch parsley
2 leeks, roughly chopped including the green part	sprig of fresh thyme
2 large onions, cut in two with the skins on	few peppercorns
2 celery stalks, roughly chopped	450g (1lb) black treacle (molasses)
2 cooking apples, roughly chopped	1 bottle of ale

1   Soak the ham for 24 hours to remove the salt, changing the water once.

2   When preparing the vegetables, wash them but do not peel or trim them before chopping. Place the vegetables and apples in a large casserole with the herbs and seasoning. Place the ham on top and add the treacle and ale, and top up with water just to cover. Bring to the boil and simmer for 4 or 5 hours.

3   Remove from the heat and leave to cool in the liquid. When completely cold lift out the ham and trim off any excess fat. You can then serve it as it is or rub the fat with brown sugar and place it in a preheated oven at 220°C (425°F/Gas 7) for 30 minutes to glaze.

Fillet of Beef with Leith Sauce

(from Aberdeen)

Aberdeen Angus cattle are synonymous with the best beef in the world and I
have therefore attributed this recipe to that region, but there are many
equally good alternatives. The beef from Highland cattle, for example, is also
excellent to cook as it is slower growing and the fat is marbled through the
meat – and, whatever our health watchdogs tell us, fat is essential for cooking
superb cuts of meat! This is a simple method of cooking top-quality beef. The
sauce is based on the wine coming into the port of Leith; this is the way that
the wine merchants would have eaten their steaks!

Serves 4
Preparation time: 45 mins

1 tsp vegetable oil
2 tsp butter
4 fillet steaks (whatever size you choose!)
salt and freshly ground black pepper

For the sauce:
½ onion, finely chopped
50g (2oz/¼ cup) butter
5 tbsp good red wine (preferably the one you
    are going to drink!)
1 clove garlic, crushed
sprig fresh thyme
1 tsp wholegrain mustard

1   Heat a frying pan and add the oil and butter. Dry the steaks, season them, and cook as
you like. Make sure that you seal them all over first in the hot oil to keep the juices in,
then reduce the heat a little and complete the cooking. Remove the steaks and keep
them warm.

2   To make the sauce: if there is any excess fat remove it from the pan, then add the onion
and half the butter and cook quickly for a couple of minutes.

3   Add the wine, garlic and thyme. Reduce by about a half and then away from the heat
swirl in the rest of the butter with the mustard. If there are any juices emanating from
the steaks at this stage add those as well! Remove the thyme sprig and serve the sauce
with the steaks.

POULTRY
AND
GAME

CASSEROLE OF GUINEA FOWL WRAPPED IN SMOKED BACON WITH RED WINE

(from Edinburgh)

This is really a version of the French *coq au vin* and the same method can be applied to any bird such as chicken or pheasant, as well as to guinea fowl. If using chicken, make sure it is organic, or at least free range, or the flavours will completely drown out its own taste. Battery chickens, like Dutch veal, are designed to carry a sauce and have no taste of their own.

Serves 4
Preparation time: 2 hours 30 mins

1 guinea fowl, about 1kg (2lb 8oz)
175 (6oz) smoked bacon rashers (slices)
salt and freshly ground black pepper
2 tbsp oil
115g (4oz/¹/₂ cup) butter

2 shallots, finely chopped
300ml (10fl oz/1¹/₄ cups) red wine
550ml (20fl oz/2¹/₂ cups) chicken stock
150ml (5fl oz/²/₃ cup) double (heavy) cream

1 Cut the bird into 8 pieces: the legs in two, two wing joints, and cut the breast bone in half. Wrap each piece in a rasher (slice) of smoked bacon, fixing with a cocktail stick (toothpick); season with salt and pepper.

2 Heat the oil with half the butter in a heavy-based pan, and brown the guinea-fowl pieces on both sides. Remove to a casserole and pour off the excess juices from the pan.

3 Put the remaining butter in the pan and add the shallots; cook until they are lightly coloured. Add the red wine and deglaze the pan, stirring to lift the bits from the pan base. Add the stock and bring to the boil.

4 Pour the stock mixture into the casserole and simmer gently for about 30 minutes. When cooked, remove the guinea fowl and keep warm.

5 Strain the stock into a clean pan and boil rapidly to reduce by half. Add the cream and simmer gently until the stock begins to take on a sauce-like quality.

6 Remove the cocktail sticks (toothpicks) from the guinea fowl and serve with the sauce poured over the top.

Pheasant and
Wild Mushroom Ragout

(from Argyll)

Pheasant has become so much of a feature of Scotland that, although it is not
indigenous, it is effectively farmed on many estates. The shooting season
starts in September. Wild mushrooms are also available at this time and the
two make an excellent combination.

Serves 4
Preparation time: 30 mins

olive oil
salt and freshly ground black pepper
4 pheasant breast fillets (halves), skinned and
    cut into dice
12 shallots, peeled and halved
2 cloves garlic, crushed
85g (3oz) wild mushrooms, sliced

200ml (7fl oz/scant 1 cup) chicken stock
115ml (4fl oz/$^1/_2$ cup) port
sprig of fresh parsley
sprig of fresh thyme
1 bay leaf
grated lemon zest to taste
200ml (7fl oz/scant 1 cup) double (heavy) cream

1   Heat a little oil in a heavy-based pan. Season the diced pheasant breast fillets, colour
    quickly in the hot oil, remove from the pan, and set aside.

2   Add the shallots to the pan and fry them quickly to colour a little, add the garlic and
    mushrooms, and cook gently for 5 minutes. Add the stock, port, herbs and lemon zest,
    and cook until the liquid is reduced a little.

3   When the shallots are nearly cooked – you should be able to pierce them with a sharp
    knife – add the cream. Reduce to thicken, then return the meat to the pan and allow to
    cook for only a few minutes to keep the meat tender. Remove the herbs and bay leaf
    before serving. If the sauce seems a little thick, add a little water.

EDINBURGH

How to put the capital into a regional context in gastronomic terms? Nothing is grown in the city, but today a farmers' market is once more helping to remind its inhabitants of the richness of produce, in terms of both variety and quality, that is available from the surrounding countryside while at the same time renewing a tradition that is very much a part of the city's history – as evidenced by street names like Cowgate or Grassmarket.

But Edinburgh kitchens have also benefited for many centuries from imports and influences from much further afield, especially from France, Scotland's partner in the 'auld alliance'. Indeed, I would go further and suggest that the trade in both goods and ideas may have flowed both ways. What the French call *pot au feu* is very reminiscent of a whole range of 'one-pot' dishes that Scots have been cooking for centuries, so who's to say they did not get the idea from us? What is undeniable, though, is that from the time of the Renaissance onwards the French wines and spices, and no doubt the French courtiers and diplomats, landed at the port of Leith gave Edinburgh a cosmopolitan sophistication that was unique in Scotland. Today, if you visit the excellent Vintners' Rooms restaurant you can see the room, still lit by candles, where the barrels of wine from Bordeaux were auctioned off; and if you visit the The National Trust for Scotland's Georgian House in Charlotte Square, you can see one of the kitchens where the elaborate dishes to accompany those wines would have been prepared.

In short, the city's eating habits, as well as its culture, manners and fashions, owed much to those of other European capitals and most of the dishes in this book which I have attributed to Edinburgh are, in fact, imports. It should be added that this cosmopolitan atmosphere had its drawbacks – Edinburgh hotels were some of the last to preserve the custom (which I find both irritating and pretentious) of writing their menus exclusively in French, even if the dish in question owed more to Dumfries than Dijon!

Later, Italian and other immigrants added to the variety available. In Valvona and Crolla, for example, Edinburgh has what must be one of the most mouth-watering shops in Britain, offering the finest Italian cheese, wine and meats; and one of the best chefs currently working in the city, Tony Singh, is a Sikh whose restaurant, Oloroso, serves dishes in which the best Scottish produce is combined with influences from the subcontinent.

The carefully preserved kitchens in the basement of The Georgian House in Charlotte Square,
belonging to The National Trust for Scotland.

CHICKEN HOWTOWDIE

(from Edinburgh)

Another delicious dish which transcends the raw materials; the idea of using
the livers for gravy works so well and does all the thickening without any
flour! The colours also are great. 'Howtowdie' was the name for a young hen
that had not yet produced any eggs.

Serves 4
Preparation time: 3 hours

1 roasting chicken, about 2kg (4lb 8oz)
175g (6oz/³/₄ cup) butter
8 shallots, peeled
550ml (20fl oz/2 ¹/₂ cups) chicken stock
6 black peppercorns
pinch of mace
2 whole cloves
1 kg (2lb) fresh spinach
1 chicken liver (optional)
2 tbsp double (heavy) cream
salt and freshly ground black pepper

For the stuffing:
50g (2oz/1 cup) fresh breadcrumbs
1 small shallot, peeled and chopped
1 tsp chopped fresh tarragon
1 tsp chopped fresh parsley
3 tbsp milk
salt and freshly ground black pepper

1   Preheat the oven to 180°C (350°F/Gas 4).

2   Mix together all the ingredients for the stuffing. With your fingers, gently pull the skin
    of the chicken away from the flesh and press the stuffing under the skin as far up as you
    can, covering the legs and breast.

3   In a large casserole, which will hold the chicken with the lid on, heat half the butter
    and, when it foams, brown the chicken on all sides. Remove the chicken with a slotted
    spoon and set aside.

4   Add the shallots to the casserole and cook until golden brown. Return the chicken to
    the casserole and add the stock and spices. Cover and cook in the oven for about 1
    hour–1 hour 30 minutes.

5   Wash the spinach and blanch by putting it in boiling water for 2 minutes, then drain
    and transfer to cold water to refresh it and halt the cooking.

6 When the chicken is cooked, remove it from the casserole and keep it warm. Drain off the stock into a clean pan and let it cool a little. Take a little of the stock and liquidize it with 25g (1oz/2 tbsp) of the butter, the cream and the chicken livers, if using. Return to the remaining stock, and check for seasoning; reheat but do not let it boil.

7 Take the drained spinach, squeeze out the excess water; heat the remaining butter in a pan and cook the spinach quickly with lots of salt and pepper. Serve the chicken with the spinach and shallots, and the sauce poured over the top of the bird.

PIGEONS A LA TOSCANA

(from Fife)

This is a recipe given to me by Elly Crichton Stuart of Falkland Palace and is taken from the family cookery book, *The Cooks' Cook Book*.

Serves 4
Preparation time: 2 hours

4 pigeons
6 tbsp olive oil
4 cloves garlic, crushed
salt and freshly ground black pepper

115g (4oz/1 cup) grated Parmesan cheese
115g (4oz/2 cups) fresh breadcrumbs
¼ tsp curry powder
pinch of cayenne

1 Preheat the oven to 180°C (350°F/Gas 4).

2 Dry the pigeons. Heat 4 tbsp of the olive oil in a large, heavy-based casserole over high heat, and brown the pigeons all over. Lower the heat, add the garlic, and season with salt and pepper.

3 Cover the casserole and cook in the oven for 1 hour. Remove from the oven.

4 Increase the oven temperature to 200°C (400°F/Gas 6). Mix the cheese with the breadcrumbs, curry powder and cayenne; sprinkle over the birds and drizzle with the remaining olive oil. Roast in oven for 12 minutes, uncovered, to crisp the coating, then serve.

CIVET OF VENISON

(from Fife; *see photograph overleaf*)

Another of the dishes popular with the Crichton Stuart family came from Jane Grigson and was used for venison – unsurprisingly, given the long history of hunting at Falkland Palace. With the excellent venison now available from the farm of John and Nicola Fletcher near Auchtermuchty it still maintains a regional flavour. This may seem quite old-fashioned, but very often original recipes are the best. My only alteration would be to cook the main body of the civet in a moderate oven and not on the stove top as suggested here; I believe it provides a more even cooking and also prevents some drying-out of the meat which, with such a lean meat as venison, is quite important.

Serves 8
Preparation time: 3 hours + overnight marinading

1.5kg (3lb 4oz) stewing venison, trimmed and diced, preferably from the shoulder or topside

For the marinade:
375ml (13fl oz/1 ²/₃ cups) red wine
1 onion, sliced
3 tbsp brandy
3 tbsp olive oil
salt and freshly ground black pepper

For the sauce:
50g (2oz/¼ cup) butter
225g (8oz) piece of streaky bacon cut into lardons, strips about 2cm (³/₄ in) long
2 large onions, peeled and chopped
1 large carrot, peeled and diced
large clove garlic, crushed
2 tbsp plain (all-purpose) flour
stock
bay leaf and sprig fresh thyme
200g (7oz) button mushrooms, sliced

For the garnish:
225g (8oz/1 cup) butter
2 tsp caster (superfine) sugar
24 small onions or shallots
stock
24 small button mushrooms
salt and freshly ground black pepper
8 slices white bread
chopped fresh parsley

1 Mix the marinade ingredients together in a large bowl, add the meat and mix in well. Leave in a cool place overnight.

2 Make the sauce: melt the butter in a large casserole and brown the bacon strips, then add the onions and carrot and cook until lightly browned. Remove the meat from the

marinade and allow it to drain thoroughly; add the meat and garlic to the casserole. Sprinkle on the flour and mix in well.

3   Strain the marinade and add to the casserole, discarding the sliced onion. Add enough stock to cover along with the herbs and mushrooms. Cover and simmer until it is cooked, about 1 hour 30 minutes–2 hours. (The dish can be cooked to this point and left until required – a couple of days if necessary.)

4   Reheat the civet gently if it has been allowed to cool. Prepare the garnish. Melt 50g (2oz/$^1/_4$ cup) of the butter with the sugar in a heavy pan. Turn the small onions in this until they are well coated then add enough stock to cover them. Boil rapidly to allow the moisture to evaporate, leaving the cooked onions nicely coated in caramel. Take care not to burn them – shake the pan gently as the process continues.

5   Heat a further 50g (2oz/$^1/_4$ cup) of the butter in another pan and cook the mushroom until lightly browned; season. Finally, cut the bread into triangles and fry in the remaining butter until crisp and brown.

6   Arrange the civet in a large hot serving dish, and put the mushrooms and caramelized onions on top so they look a part of the dish without disappearing! Place the croutons around the edge and sprinkle the whole with parsley.

KINGDOM OF FIFE PIE

(from Fife)

The original recipe for this puts the pieces of rabbit into the pie raw, I first cook them outwith the pie, otherwise it can be difficult to get the meat off the bone. I have also found with recipes using pork that it often does not provide a strong enough flavour, but then I realized that, of course, the original recipe would have used real wild boar, which would have had a gamier flavour! There was a considerable prejudice against pork in Scotland and 'pork eaters' was a term of contempt for the English! However, pigs were kept, though their meat was mostly pickled and exported. I suggest ham for this dish.

Serves 4
Preparation time: 2 hours

2 small rabbits, each cut into 6 joints
1 tbsp olive oil
2 hard-boiled eggs, quartered
350g (12oz) diced ham
salt and freshly ground black pepper
grated nutmeg
350g (12oz) puff pastry
flour for dusting
1 egg mixed with a splash of milk, for glazing

For the forcemeat balls:
2 rabbit livers
85g (3oz/1½ cups) soft white breadcrumbs
25g (1oz) diced bacon
1 tsp chopped fresh parsley
¼ tsp each chopped fresh thyme and marjoram
salt and freshly ground black pepper
1 egg

1   Make the forcemeat. Whiz all the ingredients except the egg together in a food processor until smooth and fine. Add the egg and whiz to combine. Roll the mixture into small balls and chill to firm them up.

2   Place the foreleg pieces of rabbit in a large pan and cover with water. Simmer for about 1 hour to make a stock.

3   Heat the olive oil in a large pan, and brown the saddle and leg pieces; add some of the stock, cover and cook over a low heat for about 30 minutes.

4   Preheat the oven to 220°C (425°F/Gas 7).

5   Remove the saddle and leg pieces from the stock and, when cool enough to handle, remove the meat from the bones. Place the meat in a pie dish and add the hard-boiled

96

eggs along with the diced ham and forcemeat balls. Season with salt, pepper and nutmeg. Add enough stock to one-third fill the dish.

6 Roll out the puff pastry on a floured surface, and cover the pie dish; brush with the egg wash to glaze. Bake in the oven for 15 minutes until the pastry sets, then reduce the heat to 180°C (350°F/Gas 4) and cook for another 15 minutes until the pastry is cooked and the pie heated through.

STOVED CHICKEN

(from Edinburgh)

Taken from the French word '*étuve*', meaning to cook in its own juices.
And that, of course, is also where our own stovies (page 82) get their name.

Serves 4
Preparation time: 3 hours

1 chicken, about 2.25kg (5lb), cut into 8 pieces, skin removed
115g (4oz/$\frac{1}{2}$ cup) butter, plus extra for greasing
2 large onions, peeled and sliced
550g–1kg (1lb 4oz–2lb 4oz) potatoes, sliced

salt and freshly ground black pepper
550–850ml (20fl oz–30fl oz/2$\frac{1}{2}$ cups–3$\frac{3}{4}$ cups) chicken stock
3 tbsp fresh parsley, chopped

1 Preheat the oven to 140°C (275°F/Gas 1).

2 Dry the chicken joints on kitchen paper (paper towels). Melt half the butter in a large pan, brown the chicken pieces, remove, and set aside.

3 In the same pan, sweat the onions until they colour slightly and soften.

4 Grease the insides of a large casserole. Put a layer of potato slices on the bottom, then a layer of onion, season with salt and pepper, and dot with butter. Next put a layer of chicken and then season.

5 Continue with the layers, finishing with a layer of potatoes on the top and a final dot of butter.

6 Pour three-quarters of the stock over, and cover. Cook in the oven for at least 2 hours. If it seems to be drying out add the remaining stock. When cooked, sprinkle with the chopped parsley.

FILLET OF VENISON WITH BEETROOT AND GHERKINS

(from Fife)

This is a simple but rich dish based around the classic game garnish of beetroot and gherkins. The fillet of venison is the piece tucked under the saddle and is the most tender cut. If you can't get the fillet then a piece of loin will do, or haunch steaks.

Serves 4
Preparation time: 45 mins

450g (1lb) fillet of venison
salt and freshly ground black pepper
1 tbsp olive oil
50g (2oz/¹/₄ cup) butter

175g (6oz) cooked, peeled beetroot (beets)
50g (2oz) gherkins
3 tbsp red wine
115ml (4fl oz/¹/₂ cup) dark stock

1 Dry the fillet thoroughly and season with salt and pepper. Heat a pan and add the oil and half the butter; when very hot place the fillet in the pan carefully and brown all over. Reduce the heat, cover, and cook gently for 10 minutes.

2 Meanwhile, cut the beetroot (beets) into slices about 0.5cm (¹/₄ in) thick. Then cut these slices into thin matchsticks. Do the same with the gherkins.

3 Remove the meat from the pan and keep it warm. Pour away the excess fat from the pan. Add the beetroot (beets) to the pan with the gherkins and stir around in the juices. Add the wine and evaporate by fast boiling, and then add the stock and reduce by half. Remove the pan from the heat and swirl in the remaining butter to thicken the sauce slightly; set aside.

4 Slice the venison fillet at an angle and divide between 4 serving plates. Pile the beetroot mix on top and drizzle the sauce around the meat.

Roast Grouse with Celeriac Puree and Brambles

(from Argyll; see title page)

I am very fond of grouse but don't eat it very often; in fact the best grouse I ever ate came not from Scotland, but from the Duke of Westminster's estates and was served at the River House, Poulton Le Fylde in Lancashire. Bill Scott had cooked it to perfection. The secret is not to let the breast meat dry out. I like the combination of the fruit with the flavour of the bird and the creamy texture and nuttiness of the celeriac.

Serves 4
Preparation time: 1 hour 30 mins

4 young grouse
4 rashers (slices) bacon
150ml (5fl oz/²/₃ cup) red wine
150g (5oz/1 cup) blackberries (brambles)
50g (2oz/¹/₄ cup) butter
salt and freshly ground black pepper

For the celeriac (celery root) purée:
1 celeriac (celery root)
1 lemon
2 potatoes
salt and freshly ground black pepper
300ml (10fl oz/1¹/₄ cups) double (heavy) cream

1   Prepare the celeriac purée; peel the celeriac with a small sharp knife, cutting round it from the top or, if that is difficult, cut it into quarters and then peel off the skin. Cut into smallish chunks and put into a large pan and immediately cover with cold water as it can discolour if exposed to the air. Cut the lemon in half and put into the pan as well: this helps to keep the celeriac white. Peel the potatoes and cut into similar chunks, and add them to the pan as well. (The potatoes help to provide texture.)

2   Bring to the boil and cover with a circle of greaseproof (waxed) paper to stop the celeriac coming out of the water. Simmer for about 20 minutes until tender.

3   Meanwhile, preheat the oven to 200°C (400°F/Gas 6).

4   Wipe the grouse and place them in a roasting pan. Place the rashers of bacon over the breasts of the birds. Roast in the oven for 10 minutes, then remove the bacon and pour in the wine. Return to the oven for 10 minutes, baste the birds with the juices, and cook for another 5 minutes. Remove the birds from the pan and keep them warm.

5   Drain the celeriac thoroughly, discard the lemon halves, and return to the pan to dry out still further over a low heat. Do not allow to burn! When really dry, allow to cool

slightly and purée in a food processor – alternatively mash by hand, but the texture is better done in the machine.

6   Pour the cream into a large pan and reduce by half, add the celeriac purée and stir to mix; season with salt and pepper. Keep warm.

7   Add a little water to the roasting pan and simmer gently to deglaze. Strain into a saucepan, add the brambles, and simmer to just soften the fruit but not to a purée. Remove from the heat and swirl in the butter; check the seasoning.

8   Serve the grouse with the celeriac purée, and with the bramble sauce separately.

Smoored Chicken

(from Edinburgh)

Serves 4
Preparation time: 1 hour

2 young chickens (poussins), about 450g (1lb) each
salt and freshly ground black pepper
175g (6oz/³/₄ cup) butter, melted

2 tsp mustard powder
3 tbsp milk
3 tbsp fresh breadcrumbs

1   Preheat the grill (broiler) for at least 10 minutes.

2   Cut the chickens through the backbone using a pair of heavy-duty kitchen scissors. Wipe the chicken and then dry with kitchen paper (paper towels). Place the chicken, skin side down, on the a grill (broiler) rack, season, and brush with some of the melted butter.

3   Grill (broil) until the chicken begins to colour, about 5 minutes. Turn them over and cook the other side for another 5 minutes; the fat should start to come out.

4   Mix the mustard with the milk and paint this over the skin and either continue to cook under the grill (broiler) at a lower heat, or alternatively in the preheated oven at 190°C (375°F/Gas 5), for 15-20 minutes. When just ready, increase the heat of the grill (broiler), sprinkle the breadcrumbs over the chicken, drizzle the remaining butter over the top, and brown lightly.

ROAST VENISON

(from Argyll)

Serves 8

Preparation time: 45 mins + 2 days marinading + cooking time

1 haunch of venison, about 3kg (6lb 8oz)	**For the marinade:**	**For the sauce:**
2 tbsp olive oil	4 tbsp olive oil	1 tbsp plain (all-purpose) flour
25g (1oz/2 tbsp) butter	2 carrots, peeled and sliced	15g (½oz/1 tbsp) butter, softened
225g (8oz) bacon, diced	1 onion, peeled and sliced	150ml (5fl oz/⅔ cup) port
	1 bottle (75ml) red wine	1 tbsp rowanberry jelly
	2 cloves garlic, crushed	salt and freshly ground black pepper
	1 bay leaf	
	10 black peppercorns	
	1 sprig fresh rosemary	
	2 juniper berries	

1 For the marinade, heat the olive oil over a low heat, and cook the carrots and onion without colouring them; transfer to a large non-metallic container that will hold the venison. Add the other marinade ingredients. Put the haunch in and leave to marinate in a cool place for 2 days, turning regularly.

2 Preheat the oven to 170°C (325°F/Gas 3).

3 When ready to cook, remove the haunch and dry with kitchen paper (paper towels). Put a large casserole, into which the haunch will fit with a lid, onto a high heat and add the oil and butter. Brown the bacon and then the haunch, browning it all over.

4 Meanwhile, in another pan, reduce the marinade by half by boiling it rapidly and then strain it over the haunch. Cover and cook in the oven for 30 minutes per 450g (1lb). When cooked, remove the haunch, and keep warm, covered in foil so that it does not dry out.

5 Strain off the casserole juices into a clean pan and boil rapidly. Make a 'beurre manie' by mixing the flour and butter together and then whisking into the boiling liquor. Simmer until the sauce is reduced by half and thickened. Add the port and the rowanberry jelly, check for seasoning, and serve. A haunch looks splendid presented at the table if you feel confident about carving it. The less brave can take slices in advance and serve with a little sauce over the top to keep the meat moist and hot. Serve the rest of the sauce separately.

Vegetables
and
Grains

RAGGED JACK AND SOY

(from Highlands)

Kale is obviously very much a part of the Scottish tradition, with its frequent references to 'kailyards'. 'Kale' was in fact used to describe cabbage – or something green at any rate! I have since discovered that there are at least three types of kale: curly, asparagus and ragged jack, the last having quite thin leaves with ragged edges rather like oak leaf lettuce in shape. All kales have a strong flavour and if you are not a real greens fan then you probably shouldn't try this, but it is delicious! Prepare the kale by stripping off the leaves from the tougher stalks and either tearing them up into small pieces or shredding them into smallish bite-size pieces, then wash thoroughly.

Serves 4
Preparation time: 10 mins

175g (6oz/4 cups) prepared ragged jack (kale)   1 tbsp soya sauce
2 tsp butter

1   To prepare the kale, wash and pat dry, then remove the centre stalk.

2   Heat a pan on a high heat and add the butter; as it melts toss in the kale and mix through to coat in butter and heat through, but keep it moving so it does not burn. As it wilts pour in the soya sauce and toss through. Test for doneness; it should still have a bit of a crunch.

3   Serve immediately.

ASPARAGUS WITH FONDUE BUTTER

(from Aberdeen)

As I am writing this the asparagus season is almost upon us and I have a dinner to cook at Myres this weekend which will include asparagus. I have just spoken to Sandy Pattullo who says he is expecting a good crop. I love asparagus. My first real introduction to it was in Evesham, the home of English asparagus, where in the season every pub served asparagus with butter, a fondue butter or cold with a vinaigrette - fabulous! Sadly Scottish pubs don't seem to have cottoned on to this idea but the Patullos' asparagus grown near Glamis is worth the wait - make on, it's only a six-week season! Personally I don't eat asparagus unless it is Scottish or English.

A small word of warning, remember it is the tips which are the delicacy. More than once I have had a plate returned from the restaurant with everything eaten … except a neat row of tips! Don't allow pride to get in the way of enjoyment: if you don't know which bit to eat then ask! That applies to anything!

Serves 4
Preparation time: 30 mins

40 asparagus spears
1 litre (35fl oz/4 ^{1}/$_2$ cups) water
15g (^{1}/$_2$ oz) coarse salt
2 tbsp double (heavy) cream

225g (9oz/1 cup plus 2 tbsp) cold butter, cut in
    pieces
1 tbsp lemon juice
salt and freshly ground black pepper

1   Wash the asparagus spears and trim the bases off evenly. It is not necessary to peel asparagus unless it is very large. Either trim to about 10cm (4in) lengths, and use the rest for soup, or leave the stems on to make it easier to hold while eating, whichever you prefer.

2   Bring the water to the boil, add salt, and plunge the asparagus into it. Cook for about 7 minutes or until you can just spear a stem with a knife. Remove the asparagus with a slotted spoon and keep it warm.

3   Transfer the asparagus cooking water into a small pan, and boil to reduce the liquid by one half. Add the cream and return to the boil. Remove from the heat, swirl in the butter, add the lemon juice, and season. Heat through but do not allow to boil. Place the spears on 4 plates and pour the sauce over the tips.

LEEK AND SMOKED BACON RISOTTO

(from Edinburgh)

And here is a real risotto - but using Scottish produce, in the shape of
Musselburgh leeks, those wonderful specimens, long on green and short on
white but stunning in flavour, and smoked bacon.

Serves 4-6
Preparation time: 50 mins

1.5 litres (53fl oz/6 ½ cups) chicken stock
2 tbsp unsalted butter
50g (2oz) smoked bacon, cut into small
    'lardons', strips about 2cm (³/₄in) long
2 leeks, cut into dice

400g (14oz/2 cups) Arborio rice
115ml (4fl oz/½ cup) dry white wine
1 tbsp olive oil
50g (2oz/½ cup) Parmesan cheese
salt and freshly ground black pepper

1   Heat the stock to boiling point and keep just simmering.

2   In a heavy-based pan, melt the butter over a medium heat and add the bacon; cook until
    lightly browned. Add the leeks and cook gently until softened.

3   Add the rice and stir well until well mixed. Add the wine and stir until it has been
    absorbed.

4   Now begin to add the stock, a ladleful at a time, stirring constantly and making sure that
    the liquid is all absorbed before adding the next ladle. The rice should be tender but
    still firm to the bite. If you need more liquid use a little water.

5   Remove the risotto from the heat and stir in the olive oil and cheese. Check the
    seasoning and serve.

ABERDEEN, ANGUS
AND PERTHSHIRE

Aberdeen, being the place of my birth, brings to mind so many memories, in spite of the fact that I only lived there for four years. My father was a parish minister and we lived in the heart of a farming community, surrounded by some of the finest beef and dairy cattle in the country, including the famous Aberdeen Angus, a breed still seen as being synonymous with quality, though today there are several other breeds which can give the black cattle a run for their money

As a child I can remember the word 'piece' being used for the sandwich or snack that the farm labourers would have mid-morning. It came originally from the idea of taking cold porridge out onto the hills. After the porridge was eaten at breakfast the remains would be turned out into the porridge drawer where it would cool and before the men went out onto the hills they would cut a 'piece' from it to sustain themselves during the day! All that has gone now, but the pace of life is still perhaps a little slower than elsewhere in Scotland and, in spite of the oil boom in Aberdeen itself, I always feel the people have a certain closeness to the land.

The rich land of the coastal plain still produces fine potatoes and grain is grown for whisky as well as for flour that goes into the legendary buttery rowies. In my childhood, oats, too, were widely grown. Over on the coast north of Aberdeen in the village of Cullen a soup was created from the traditional staples of potatoes and smoked haddock; further south into Angus we find more smoked produce. At Auchmithie the first smokies were produced. Today Peterhead remains one of the country's major fishing ports, though sadly declining as fish stocks in the North Sea dwindle and the EU imposes ever stricter regulations.

*Top quality vegetables are still at the heart of
much of Scotland's agriculture.*

SUMMER VEGETABLE STEW

(from Edinburgh)

I have attributed this recipe to Edinburgh only because I like to remember the great markets for the fresh produce which came into the city from the south. Today we have the farmers' markets and, of course, lots of organic smallholdings dotted around the edge of the city. So even in the heat of a busy August in town you can still create a sense of summer in the country with this wonderful salad/stew.

Serves 4
Preparation time: 45 mins

50g (2oz/¹/₄ cup) butter
4 spring onions (scallions), quartered
1 clove garlic, crushed
115g (4oz) courgettes (zucchini), cut in lengths

115g (4oz) green peas
115g 4oz broad (fava) beans
2 little gem lettuces, quartered
1 tsp finely chopped fresh tarragon

1   Heat half the butter in a frying pan, and fry the onions and garlic gently until soft.

2   Add the courgettes (zucchini), peas and beans, with a splash of water to help steam them. Season and cook gently for a few minutes.

3   Add the lettuce and allow to warm through. Stir in the remaining butter and the tarragon. Serve with a bottle of something cold and pink!

BARLEY RISOTTO

(from Edinburgh)

I had to include this idea, which takes an Italian classic and turns it into something Scottish. A barley risotto is not so good as a rice one, but it makes an excellent and unusual accompaniment to grilled lamb. As with a rice risotto, you can of course add other flavours and ingredients, but here is a basic method. You need to remember that barley takes longer to cook than rice.

Serves 4
Preparation time: 1 hour

550ml (20fl oz/2¹/₂ cups) chicken stock
85g (3oz/¹/₃ cup) butter
1 onion, peeled and chopped
225g (8oz) barley

2 tbsp red wine
1 tbsp olive oil
50g (2oz/¹/₂ cup) grated Bonnet cheese
chopped fresh parsley

1 Bring the stock to the boil, and keep just simmering.

2 Melt the butter in a heavy-based pan, and sweat the chopped onion. Add the barley, and stir to coat well.

3 Add the wine and stir until it is absorbed, then add a ladleful of stock and stir until it is nearly absorbed. Continue adding stock on in this way until all the stock is absorbed; the barley should be just cooked with a little 'bite' to it and the texture in the pan should be creamy.

4 Stir in the olive oil and the grated cheese. Serve with lots of fresh chopped parsley.

COLCANNON

(from Aberdeen)

I have attributed this recipe to Aberdeen but only because the original comes from a cookery book compiled by that city's Robert Gordon's Technical College and published in 1944. It is in fact a Highland dish, and sadly, as the book's author, the good Dr Ross observed, the recipe calls for all the vegetables to be boiled! So here is my version of colcannon. The only boiled bit is the potatoes!

'Kailkenny' is another such type of recipe, although it adds cream to the mixture of boiled potatoes and boiled cabbage. The name is probably a corruption of Colcannon.

Serves 4
Preparation time: 1 hour

450g (1lb) potatoes, peeled
50g (2oz/¼ cup) butter
1 tbsp olive oil
1 onion, peeled and finely chopped

225g (8oz) dark green cabbage or spring greens, shredded
salt and freshly ground black pepper

1 Boil the potatoes in a large pan of water until cooked and drain. Mash them with the butter and keep warm.

2 Heat the olive oil in a large frying pan and fry the onion until soft and lightly browned.

3 Add the cabbage and cook quickly, stirring all the time until the cabbage softens. Add the mashed potato and stir to combine and heat through. Season with salt and black pepper before serving.

TOMATO GRATIN

(from Dumfries)

Serves 4
Preparation time: 1 hour

butter, for greasing
300ml (10fl oz/1¼ cups) double (heavy) cream
2 sprigs fresh tarragon
3 beef tomatoes

salt and freshly ground black pepper
2 tbsp freshly grated Parmesan or Bonnet
 cheese

1   Preheat the oven to 220°C (425°F/Gas 7).

2   Butter a gratin dish. Put the cream and tarragon in a pan and simmer gently until the cream has reduced by half. Strain off the cream, discarding the tarragon.

3   Blanch the tomatoes in boiling water for a few seconds, then plunge into cold water. Leave to cool completely, then peel and slice into rounds.

4   Layer the tomatoes into the prepared gratin dish and season, then pour the cream over, and sprinkle on the cheese. Bake in the oven until brown, for about 15 minutes.

SALSIFY

(from Borders)

This recipe comes from the archives of the Malcolm family who lived at Langholm in the Borders. Salsify, which for years I remember coming in white boxes from Belgium, obviously found its way into the farming community of Lowland Scotland - perhaps from south of the border, since the page with the recipe has the word 'Batsford' in the corner, a reference to the family estate in England. But however the plant made its way to Scotland, I am grateful because it is delicious and too little used.

The original version reads as follows:

Boil the root until quite tender then take it out of the water, cut it up in small slices have a saucepan ready, put it in, add pepper, salt and a little cream then warm it, have the shells ready slightly buttered, then cover the shells with a fine breadcrumbs then fill them nearly full of the salsify and then cover them nicely over with breadcrumbs then put on the top a few small lumps of fresh butter and then brown them in a quick oven or before the fire.

Quite what the 'shells' are I don't know, but you could always use scallop shells! Here is my version.

Serves 4
Preparation time: 1 hour

450g (1lb) salsify
1 lemon, halved
150ml (¼ pint) double (heavy) cream

salt and freshly ground black pepper
2 tbsp soft white breadcrumbs
25g (1oz/2 tbsp) butter

1 Peel the salsify carefully, taking care not to take too much off, and put it in a stainless-steel pan with water to cover. Squeeze the lemon halves into the pan, and add them to the water to keep the vegetable white. Bring to the boil and simmer gently until tender - about 30 minutes.

2 Meanwhile, put the cream into a pan and reduce slightly, seasoning with salt and pepper.

3 When the salsify is cooked, drain, allow to cool slightly, and pat dry. Cut into lengths the size of your little finger and place in a heatproof dish. Pour the cream over, sprinkle the breadcrumbs on top, and dot with the butter. Brown under a preheated grill (broiler). Delicious as an accompaniment to lamb!

DESSERTS
AND
BAKING

APRICOT TART

(from Borders)

A delicious tart using apricots with a glaze made from the fruit as well.

Serves 4
Preparation time: 1 hour (not including blind baking)

500g (1lb 2oz/2 cups) sugar
500ml (18fl oz/2 ¼ cups) water
cinnamon stick
20 fresh apricots, cut in half and the stones
    removed
175ml (6fl oz/³/₄ cup) double (heavy) cream

115ml (4fl oz/¹/₂ cup) sour (soured) cream
2 eggs
50g (2oz/¹/₄ cup) caster (superfine) sugar
50g (2oz/¹/₄ cup) butter
sweet pastry case baked blind (see page 148)

1   Make the syrup: combine the sugar and water in a large pan, bring to the boil and skim
    the top. Add the cinnamon stick and simmer for 5 minutes. Remove the cinnamon.

2   Preheat the oven to 220°C (425°F/Gas 7).

3   Poach the apricots in the syrup until just cooked, about 10 minutes – they should still
    hold their shape. Remove the apricots and reserve the syrup.

4   Mix the two creams together, beat in the eggs, and add the sugar. Melt the butter and
    fold into the egg and cream mixture.

5   Arrange the apricots with the cut edges facing up in circles in the pastry case. Pour the
    cream mix over and place carefully in the oven. Bake for 25 minutes until just set and
    lightly browned. Leave to cool slightly before serving. If you like, reduce the sugar syrup
    down slightly then use it to glaze the tart.

BERE BANNOCKS

(from Highlands)

Bere meal comes from a form of barley which only grows successfully in the
north. It has a very distinctive flavour, making dark, nutty bannocks. I first
came across them on Orkney, where bere is still grown.

A girdle (griddle) is the old-fashioned metal plate that sat over an open fire
on which much of the baking was done in the days when there were no ovens.
My granny in Glasgow still used to bake all sorts of things on hers when I
visited her as a child. An Aga simmering plate is an ideal substitute, or just a
big heavy-based pan over a low flame on the stove will do. If all else fails put it
into the oven at 190°C (375°F/Gas 5).

Serves 4
Preparation time: 45 mins

300ml (10fl oz/1¼ cups) milk
2 tsp bicarbonate of soda (baking soda)
450g (1lb) bere meal

115g (4oz/1 cup) self-raising (self-rising) flour,
   plus extra for dusting
½ tsp salt

1 Warm the milk and add the bicarbonate of soda, mix with both the flours and the salt to
   make a pliable dough.

2 Roll out on a board with lots of flour to prevent sticking, to about 1cm (¼ in) thick and
   cut out rounds the size of a soup plate. Bake on a girdle (griddle) or in the oven until
   brown on both sides.

BLACK BUN

(from Borders)

This is a very traditional Scottish sweetmeat and is usually associated by most Scots with Hogmanay when it is eaten with a nip or two of whisky! It differs from most fruit cakes in that it is baked in a pastry case. It should be kept for several weeks to mature.

Makes about 16 slices
Preparation time: 4 hours 30 mins

For the pastry case:
225g (8oz /1 cup) butter
450g (1lb/4 cups) plain (all-
purpose) flour
1 tsp baking powder
butter for greasing

For the filling:
900g (2lb/6 cups) raisins
1.35kg (3lb/8 cups) currants
225g (8oz/2 ¼ cups) chopped
almonds
350g (12oz/3 cups) plain (all-
purpose) flour
250g (8oz/1¼ cups) soft brown
sugar

2 tsp allspice
1 tsp of ginger, cinnamon,
freshly ground black
pepper, and baking powder
1 tsp cream of tartar
1 tbsp brandy
1 beaten egg
about 150ml (5fl oz/ ²/₃ cup)
milk

1   To make the pastry case, rub the butter into the flour with the baking powder and add enough cold water mix to a stiff dough. Leave to rest and roll out to a fairly thin sheet. Grease 2 x 20cm (8 in) loaf tins and line them with the dough, reserving enough to cover the top.

2   Preheat the oven to 110°C (225°F/Gas ¹/₄).

3   Make the filling. Mix all the dry ingredients together, then mix in the brandy, egg, and enough milk to moisten the mixture. Put it into the prepared loaf tins and cover with the remaining pastry. Use the remaining milk or an egg wash (1 egg beaten with a splash of milk) to seal the top crust. Prick all over with a fork and brush with egg wash. Bake in the oven for about 3 hours. When it is cool store in an airtight tin.

BURNT CREAM

(from Aberdeen)

This pudding comes originally from Aberdeenshire. The story goes that a young man from an Aberdeen farm got a place at a Cambridge college and brought a family recipe to be tried in hall. Since he was only an undergraduate his suggestion was quickly dismissed. However, not to be deterred, the young man became a fellow of the same college and reintroduced his family pudding. Now, with his new status, it was accepted and is apparently a staple of the college, which needless to say thought that all things good in the culinary world must have a French name, hence crème brulée. I am sure our hero (as he most certainly now is) would have called it 'burnt cream'.

Sadly the French have a way of making us think they know best. Once I had a party in my restaurant who had been to France, thought they knew it all and asked for the crème brulée – hot! Now this means that our party had been in some substandard bistro where the chef couldn't be bothered to do things properly and served this classic pudding still warm from the grill! My dear guests thought that this was the right, French, way. Ah, how we chefs are tried!

Anyway, after all that, here is my recipe and, as the son of an Aberdeen manse, I might be allowed to think I am close to the real thing!

Serves 6-8
Preparation time: 40 mins + cooling time

550ml (20fl oz/2½ cups) double (heavy) cream
a few drops of vanilla essence (extract) or 2
vanilla pods, split and the seeds scraped out
but reserved

5 large egg yolks
115g (4oz/¼ cup) caster (superfine) sugar
Demerara (raw) sugar

1 Put the cream in a stainless steel pan with the vanilla essence (or the scraped out pods with the seeds), bring to boiling point, but not too quickly or else the pan base will burn. Remove from the heat and set aside to allow the vanilla to infuse.

2 Place the egg yolks into a large bowl with the caster (superfine) sugar and whisk until light and creamy. Pour the cream onto the egg mixture, whisking all the time. Wipe out the pan, and return the mixture to the pan and place over a low heat.

3 Bring very slowly to the boil, stirring all the time. As it thickens, keep away from too high a heat or else your mix will scramble.

4 When it coats the back of a spoon, continue stirring away from the heat and strain through a sieve. Pour into ramekins (6 medium ones or 8 small ones). Leave to set for at least 6 hours.

5 Just before serving, sprinkle a thin layer of Demerara (raw) sugar evenly over each one. Take care to make the layer even and thin otherwise part may be uncooked and part burned. Take a blow torch and play the flame gently over the surface to caramelize the sugar. Chill for 10 minutes before serving.

BLAEBERRY MUFFINS

(from Aberdeen)

These wonderful little berries grow all over Scotland, especially in the woods in Fife and Speyside. They do tend to be smaller than the American blueberries but I find they have a much more intense flavour. They are delicious sprinkled over yoghurt for breakfast or in a tart; but this recipe adds them to a muffin and makes a lovely tea-time treat!

Makes 10
Preparation time: 1 hour

25g (1oz/2 tbsp) butter, plus extra for greasing
225g (8oz/2 cups) self-raising (self-rising) flour
150g (5oz/^{2}/$_3$ cup) caster (superfine) sugar
1 tsp bicarbonate of soda (baking soda)
pinch of salt

pinch of ground cloves
225ml (8fl oz/1 cup) yogurt
1 egg
zest of 1 lemon
320g (11oz/2 cups) blueberries

1 Preheat the oven to 190°C (375°F/Gas 5).

2 Butter 10 muffin tins. Mix together the flour, sugar, soda, salt and ground cloves.

3 Melt the butter and beat in the yogurt, egg, and lemon zest. Stir into the dry ingredients and lastly fold the blueberries in gently. Divide between the tins and bake for about 20 minutes.

CARROT CAKE

(from Borders)

I have included this as it appears to be a favourite among the customers at many of The National Trust for Scotland's tea rooms.

Serves 6-8
Preparation time: 1 hour 30 mins

4 eggs
450g (1lb/2 ¹/₂ cups) soft brown sugar
175ml (6fl oz/³/₄ cup) vegetable oil
50ml (2fl oz/¹/₄ cup) milk
1 tsp vanilla essence (extract)
175g (6oz/1¹/₂ cup) plain (all-purpose) flour
1 tsp nutmeg
1 heaped tsp cinnamon
1 tsp bicarbonate of soda (baking soda)
large pinch of salt

115g (4oz/1¹/₃ cups) desiccated coconut
115g (4oz) grated carrot, plus extra for decoration

For the topping:
115g (4oz) icing (confectioners') sugar
225g (8oz/1 cup) cream cheese
115g (4oz/¹/₂ cup) butter
juice of ¹/₂ lemon

1   Preheat the oven to 150°C (300°F/Gas 2). Line a 25cm (10 in) cake tin with greaseproof (waxed) paper.

2   Beat together eggs, sugar, oil, milk and vanilla essence (extract).

3   Mix the flour with the nutmeg, cinnamon, bicarbonate of soda (baking soda) and salt, and sift into the egg mixture. Add the coconut and carrot. Pour the mixture into the prepared cake tin.

4   Bake for 1 hour. Pierce the cake with a skewer; if it comes out clean the cake is cooked. Leave the cake to cool in the tin for about 5 minutes, then remove and place on a wire-cooling tray.

5   For the topping: sift the icing (confectioners') sugar and beat into the cream cheese, butter and lemon juice. Spread the mixture over the cake and decorate with grated carrot around the edges.

BUTTERIES

(from Aberdeen; see photograph overleaf)

The traditional Aberdonian breakfast roll. The method is similar to that of a croissant but, frankly, even more delicious. I once stayed up all night at a party in Oxford and made a batch of these wonderful pastries. Hangovers were cleared very quickly as the smell of freshly baked butteries wafted over the sleeping party-goers! It is time that all Scots hotels abandoned the ubiquitous croissant and started serving the real thing!

Makes 16
Preparation time: 30 mins + rising time

½ tbsp dried yeast
1 tbsp soft brown sugar
390ml (15fl oz/1½ cups) warm water
500g (1lb/3 cups) strong white (bread) flour

pinch of salt
225g (8oz/1 cup) butter
115g (4 oz/½ cup) lard

1   Blend the yeast with the sugar and a little of the warm water to dissolve, then set aside.

2   Put the flour in a basin with the salt. When the yeast has begun to froth, pour it into the flour with the remaining water. Knead well to form a dough, cover and leave it in a warm place to rise.

3   Blend the butter and lard together until smooth but not liquid, and divide into three.

4   When the dough has doubled in size, push it back to its original size and knead it again. Then roll it out to a rectangle about 1cm (½ in) thick. Spread a third of the butter mixture over two-thirds of the dough.

5   Fold the other third of the dough over onto the butter, and the last third onto it, thus giving three layers. Roll this back to the original size.

6   Cover and leave to rest in a cool place for at least 40 minutes and repeat the above procedure, including leaving to rest, another two times, thus finishing the butter mixture. Cut the dough into 16 squares. Shape into rough circles by folding the edges in all the way around and place on a baking sheet.

7   Leave to rise, covered with a dry cloth, for 45 minutes.

8   Preheat the oven to 200°C (400°F/Gas 6).

9   Bake for 15 minutes until golden brown and flaky. Serve with yet more butter and marmalade and lots of coffee – you have a breakfast fit for a king!

Cloutie Dumpling

(from Borders)

A rich, dense pudding, traditionally made in a 'cloot' or cloth and then boiled
in water over the fire. Another in-the-pot dish.

Serves 8
Preparation time: 3 hours 30 mins

115g (4oz/^{1}/$_2$ cup) suet
225g (8oz/2 cups) plain (all-purpose) flour
115g (4oz/^{3}/$_4$ cup) oatmeal
85g (3oz/^{1}/$_3$ cup) sugar
1 tsp baking powder
225g (8oz/1 ^{1}/$_2$ cups) mixed sultanas and
    currants

1 tsp each of cinnamon and ginger
1 tbsp golden syrup
2 eggs, lightly beaten
3–4 tbsp milk
1 tbsp flour for a 'cloot' or cloth, or butter for
    greasing a pudding basin
hot jam and cream, to serve

1   Using your fingertips, rub the fat into the flour, and add the oatmeal, sugar and baking
    powder, fruit and spices. Mix in well, then add the syrup and eggs. Stir all together,
    using enough milk to form a firm batter.

2   If you are using a pudding cloth, it should be either a cotton or linen cloth, about 55cm
    (21 in) square. Plunge it first into boiling water, remove it carefully and lay it out, then
    sprinkle flour over it. Place the pudding mixture in the middle of the floured cloth and
    tie it up, leaving plenty of space for the pudding to expand.

3   Put an inverted plate or saucer at the bottom of a deep pan, put the dumpling in and
    cover it with boiling water, and cook for 2 ^{1}/$_2$-3 hours over a low heat.

4   If you are using a pudding basin, lightly grease the inside and put the mixture in,
    allowing at least 2.5cm (1 in) space at the top. Cover with greaseproof (waxed) paper
    and tie down well. Either place in a bain marie (water bath) with water up to the rim and
    boil over a low heat for 2 ^{1}/$_2$-3 hours, or steam over a double boiler. Turn out onto a
    warmed large plate. Serve in slices with hot jam and cream.

CRANACHAN

(from Fife)

A truly classic Scottish pudding and one which celebrates so many good things from Fife – cream, fruit, oatmeal and, of course, whisky!

Take care with the cream in this one as if it is over-whipped to start with, then by the time you come to add the fruit it will be too thick and will resemble cold porridge.

Serves 4
Preparation time: 30 mins

85g (3oz/²/₃ cup) pinhead oatmeal
550ml (20fl oz/2 ¹/₂ cups) double (heavy) cream
6 tbsp Scotch whisky

1 tbsp Scottish (heather) honey
450g (1lb/3 cups) raspberries

1   Put the oatmeal onto a baking sheet, place under a preheated grill (broiler), and toast for 3-5 minutes. Take care it does not burn. Leave to cool.

2   Lightly whip the cream with the whisky and honey, then fold in the lightly toasted oatmeal and lastly the raspberries. Spoon into tall glasses, and chill for at least 1 hour, or overnight, before serving.

DAMSON CRUMBLE

(from Borders)

Sticking to the fruit theme, crumbles are a simple way of using larger fruits which would have grown in the walled gardens of many of the houses in the Borders region. This recipe calls for damsons, but would work equally well with apples, brambles or rhubarb. The use of oatmeal in this traditional recipe adds a lovely nutty taste. The oatmeal also absorbs the juices of the fruit, creating a luscious texture to the sauce.

Serves 4
Preparation time: 1 hour

450g (1lb) stoned (pitted) damsons
50g (2oz/^{1}/$_3$ cup) soft brown sugar
1 tbsp water
juice of 1 lemon

For the crumble topping:
50g (2oz/^{1}/$_2$ cup) plain (all-purpose) flour
25g (1oz/^{1}/$_4$ cup) coarse oatmeal
50g (2oz/^{1}/$_3$ cup) soft brown sugar
50g (2oz/^{1}/$_4$ cup) butter, softened

1 Preheat the oven to 200°C (400°F/Gas 6).

2 Cook the fruit with the sugar, water and lemon juice until just softening. Place in a deep pie dish.

3 Mix together the crumble ingredients, creating a breadcrumb-like texture. Sprinkle evenly over the fruit and bake for 20 minutes or until the top is crunchy and brown.

GATEAU AUX MARRONS ET AU CHOCOLAT

(from Fife)

Another recipe enjoyed by the Lorimer family at Kellie Castle and given to me
by Monica Heyman, Hugh Lorimer's daughter.

Serves 6-8
Preparation time: 1 hour 30 mins + cooling time

For the cake:
85g (3oz) bitter (dark) chocolate
2 tsp strong black coffee
4 eggs, separated
225g (8oz/1¼ cups) caster (superfine) sugar
225g (8oz) cooked and peeled (or ready to use)
    sweet chestnuts, chopped
butter, for greasing

For the chocolate filling:
85g (3oz) bitter (dark) chocolate
2 tbsp water
2 egg yolks, beaten with sugar to taste
300ml (10fl oz/1¼ cups) double (heavy) cream

1   Preheat the oven to 190°C (375°F/Gas 5).

2   Make the cake mixture: melt the chocolate to a thick cream with a little strong black
coffee. Beat the egg yolks and sugar until white, then add the chocolate mixture. Fold in
the chestnuts. Whisk the egg whites until stiff and dry and fold into the cake mixture.

3   Line 2 shallow cake tins with well-buttered paper, pour half the mixture into each, and
bake in the oven for 30-40 minutes.

4   To make the chocolate filling: mix the chocolate and water and melt slowly over low
heat until thickened. Add the egg yolk and sugar mixture, well beaten. Stir until
smooth. Allow to cool, and stir in the cream.

5   When the cake is cool, spread one half with the chocolate filling and sandwich the two
halves together. Pour a little more chocolate filling over, to cover.

THE BORDERS

Much of this region is made up of rich, green countryside, dotted with a sprinkling of large houses and prosperous farms. Many of these still have the walled gardens which would originally have been planted with orchards and fruit bushes.

In the National Library in Edinburgh I found recipes recorded in the late seventeenth and early eighteenth century by Katharine Bruce and her family who came from Saltoun in East Lothian. Many of them are for fruit, and the range of produce and the variety of ways in which it was used are very impressive; there are recipes for raspberry and gooseberry cakes, for example, and cherries, pippins, red and white currants, plums and quinces all feature in the household's diet. Much time and ingenuity was devoted to preserving this rich summer harvest for consumption during the cold grey days of winter: invariably each long list of instructions is followed by 'Another way…' so that every square inch of paper is covered in spidery writing.

It is clear that even the well-to-do devoted much of their time to nurturing, harvesting and preserving the foodstuffs which grew in their gardens, and in the woods and fields which surrounded them. One of my favourite recipes is for 'Cattlehup' (ketchup) made from the wild mushrooms that could be gathered in the pastures in autumn.

Mushrooms, break them remarkably well [what a wonderfully expressive way of putting it!] in your hand, lay them in a broad earthen dish and put upon them as much salt as you think proper. Leave them 1 or 2 days, strain through a hair sieve or coarse cloth into a pan and boil for 20 minutes, skimming well, take off the fire, store until the next day, then back on the fire, skim again add more salt if recquissite [sic] then add common pepper, jam [?], mace, cloves, ginger and cayenne. It should taste strongly of them all, boil quickly on a clear fire for 15 minutes to allow to cook - bottle.

A contemporary (and less time-consuming) version of this recipe can be found on page 153.

The range of spices required for the 'Cattlehup' is impressive; most of these would have been imported through the port of Leith and were, perhaps, purchased in Edinburgh when surplus produce was taken into the city to be sold in one of the street markets there. These spices also found their way into the pastries, bread and cakes which were another of the region's specialities - see, for example, Black Bun (page 118), Ecclefechan Tart (page 134), Petticoat Tails (page 139) and Selkirk Bannock (page 142).

A basket of freshly picked plums glows in the late summer sunshine.

GINGERBREAD

(from Borders)

There appear to be recipes for this cake from all over the country. I have found them in books from Aberdeenshire and Speyside parish churches, from the notes in Tenement House in Glasgow and also from Ayrshire, so I have rather arbitrarily attributed this recipe to the Borders! In fact, it seems likely that gingerbread, like shortbread, was a favourite throughout our nation of bakers.

Serves 6-8
Preparation time: 3 hours + cooling and maturing

175g (6oz/³⁄₄ cup) butter, plus extra for greasing
175g (6oz/¹⁄₂ cup) golden syrup
175g (6oz/¹⁄₂ cup) black treacle (molasses)
150ml (5fl oz/²⁄₃ cup) cold water
1 tsp bicarbonate of soda (baking soda)
4 tbsp milk
350g (12oz/3 cups) plain (all-purpose) flour

1¹⁄₂ tsp ground ginger
2 level tsp cinnamon
¹⁄₄ tsp ground nutmeg
175g (6oz/1 cup) soft brown sugar
2 eggs, beaten

1   Preheat the oven to 150°C (300°F/Gas 2); butter a 23-25cm (9-10 in) cake pan and line with greaseproof (waxed) paper.

2   Melt the butter, syrup, treacle (molasses) and water together and leave to cool. Mix the bicarbonate of soda (baking soda) with milk.

3   Add the syrup mixture to all the dry ingredients, then the beaten eggs. Add the milk mixture and blend in thoroughly. Pour into the prepared tin

4   Bake for 1 hour 20 minutes-2 hours until the cake is lightly risen and firm in the centre. To test, insert a skewer or thin knife in the gingerbread: it should be clean and not sticky.

5   Leave to cool in the tin and store wrapped in foil for a couple of days. I like my gingerbread with butter spread on it!

GLAYVA PARFAIT

(from Dumfries)

I want to include an idea of Nick Nairn's for a sauce to accompany the parfait:
he uses Armagnac with Agen prunes and an infusion of Earl Grey tea.

600ml (20 fl oz) stock syrup
1 tbsp Earl Grey tea leaves
20 Agen Prunes
2 tsp Armagnac

Leave the prunes to soak in water overnight and remove the stones. Bring the syrup
to the boil and add the tea leaves and leave to infuse for 5 minutes. Strain through
a sieve, add the prunes, the Armagnac and a little lemon juice, then leave to cool.
Make the parfait as in the recipe below but pour it into dariole moulds. When
ready to serve, turn the parfaits out and place the prunes around the plate with
the syrup drizzled around. Very stylish – very Nick Nairn!

Serves 4
Preparation time: 40 mins + freezing time

115g (4oz/ ¹/₂ cup) caster (superfine) sugar
6 tbsp water
6 egg yolks

3 tbsp Glayva (Scotch whisky) liqueur
225ml (8fl oz/1 cup) double (heavy) cream

1 In a small saucepan, place the sugar and the water; simmer for a couple of minutes until
   the bubbles start to get slightly smaller.

2 Put the egg yolks into a bowl and place it over a pan of simmering water. Whisk the egg
   yolks and when they are light in texture add the boiling sugar. Whisk until the mixture
   forms a ribbon and then remove from the heat and continue to whisk until it is cooled.
   Use a hand electric whisk, as it takes some time to whisk until cool. Better still, transfer
   the bowl to an electric mixer.

3 Add the liqueur, then lightly whip the cream and fold into the mixture. Pour into
   individual serving dishes and freeze.

GROSER FOOL

(from Fife)

The Scots word for gooseberries. At the time of year when gooseberries ripen
elderflowers also come out and you can flavour the fool with them as well. Just add a head
of the flowers to the gooseberries as you cook them for a delightful scented flavour.

Serves 4
Preparation time: 20 mins + time to cook the fruit

450g (1lb) gooseberries
85g (3oz/^{1}/$_3$ cup) caster (superfine) sugar
pastry cream (see page 149) or cold custard

whipped cream
shortbread, to serve (optional)

1 Cook the fruit in a non-aluminium pan (aluminium tends to taint the flavour of acidic
   fruits) with the sugar and a splash of water. Allow to cool and purée in a food processor,
   then push through a sieve. This will give a you a deep green, smooth purée.

2 Combine 2 parts of the purée with 1 part of pastry cream or cold custard and then fold
   in 1 part of lightly whipped cream. Serve with shortbread, if you like.

Editor's note: instructions for pastry cream are in Tayberry Tart.

ECCLEFECHAN TART

(from Borders)

The Borders region is famous for this kind of baking, using fruit, dried or
otherwise. Recipes must have varied from house to house, often dictated by
what was grown or produced locally. The base uses a simple sweet pastry
(see page 148) which can be used for endless variety of sweet tarts.

Serves 4
Preparation time: 1 hour 15 mins

sweet pastry (see page 148)
flour, for dusting
50g (2oz/^{1}/$_4$ cup) butter
85g (3oz/^{1}/$_3$ cup) soft brown sugar

1 egg
2 tsp white wine vinegar
115g (4oz/^{3}/$_4$ cup) sultanas
25g (1oz/^{1}/$_4$ cup) broken walnuts

1   Preheat the oven to 190°C (375°F/Gas 5).

2   Roll out the sweet pastry on floured surface. Line a 20cm (8 in) tart pan with the pastry and bake blind for 20 minutes.

3   Melt the butter and mix with the sugar and egg; stir in the vinegar, sultanas and walnuts. Spread into the pastry case and bake for 30 minutes.

HOT LEMON TEACAKE [LISSANOURE]

(from Fife)

Another recipe provided by Monica Heyman of Kellie Castle, it should be eaten hot and running with butter. If you like a seedy cake, reduce the lemon by half and replace with a teaspoon of caraway seeds.

Serves 4
Preparation time: 1 hour

115g (4oz/¹/₂ cup) butter, plus extra for greasing
115g (4oz/¹/₂ cup) caster (superfine) sugar
2 eggs, separated

grated zest and juice of 1 lemon
115g (4oz/1 cup) self-raising flour

1   Preheat the oven to 180°C (350°F/Gas 4).

2   Cream the butter, and beat in the sugar thoroughly. Add the egg yolks with the lemon zest and juice and 1-2 tbsp of the flour.

3   Whip the egg whites to a firm froth and fold into the mixture with the remaining flour. Turn at once into a shallow greased and floured cake tin and bake in the oven for 20-30 minutes. Split while still hot and butter lavishly.

Lemon Posset with Brambles and Passion Fruit

(from Fife)

A simple old-fashioned pudding combined with a delicious fruity sauce.

Serves 6
Preparation time: 45 mins + setting time

1.2 litres (40fl oz/5 cups) double (heavy) cream
thinly peeled rind and juice of 2 lemons
3 leaves gelatine
150ml (5fl oz/²/₃ cup) cold milk
150g (5oz/1 cup) icing (confectioners') sugar

For the brambles and passion fruit:
4 passion fruit
115g (4oz/1 cup) brambles
50g (2oz/¹/₄ cup) caster (superfine) sugar

1   Pour 900ml (32fl oz/4 cups) of the cream into a pan and add the lemon rind. Bring to the boil and allow to simmer very gently until reduced by a third – about 15 minutes. Set aside.

2   In a small pan, soak the gelatine in the cold milk until it is soft. Then gently heat it until the gelatine dissolves. Add this to the cooling cream and strain.

3   When the cream mixture has nearly cooled, whip the remaining cream with the icing (confectioners') sugar until it just begins to hold. Fold it into the cooled cream mixture and gently stir in the lemon juice. Pour into 6 ramekins and leave in the refrigerator until set – about 6 hours.

4   Cut the passion fruit in half and scoop out the seeds with a teaspoon. In a stainless-steel pan, put the brambles and the caster (superfine) sugar and, over a low heat, stir gently until the brambles soften and cook in the sugar. Add the passion-fruit seeds and stir to combine. Keep the mixture warm.

5   To serve, turn out the possets on to 6 plates by dipping the bases of the ramekins in warm water for a few minutes; they should just ease out as they soften. Strew the bramble and passion fruit mixture around the outside and serve.

OATMEAL PRALINE ICE CREAM

(from Dumfries)

The Italian community is a large one in Scotland, especially in Glasgow with its wonderful ice cream parlours. However, we are lucky enough to have the most exciting of Italian delis, called Valvona and Crolla, in Edinburgh. I can remember going in as a child with my mother and the smell of fresh coffee, the sound of grand opera, the sight of salamis and cheeses of every size and shape hanging from the ceiling still lives with me. Today, sadly, the dead hand of the environmental health officer has curtailed some of the showy displays with everything now packaged or behind bulletproof glass! Nevertheless it is still an inspiring place to visit. Once you have had your fill of the Georgian House and Gladstone's Land then take the trip to Elm Row and stock up!

This recipe is a real hybrid! But then I suppose most recipes are and whether or not it's traditional the oatmeal does make a very unusual ice cream. You need to prepare the oatmeal first; I find a pinhead type is the best. Allow it to cool and then put it all together.

Serves 4
Preparation time: 45 mins + freezing time

6 egg whites
250g (9oz/1¼ cups) caster (superfine) sugar
200ml (7fl oz/scant 1 cup) double (heavy) cream
300ml/10fl oz/1¼ cups) single (light) cream

For the oatmeal crunch:
115g (4oz/½ cup) caster (superfine) sugar
2 tbsp water
115g (4oz/¾ cup) pinhead oatmeal

1 Prepare the oatmeal. Bring the sugar to the boil with the water in a pan. When the sugar begins to turn golden brown, stir in the oatmeal and pour onto an oiled baking tray. Cool then crush into small pieces using a rolling pin or a pestle and mortar.

2 Whisk the egg whites and sugar in a bowl over a pan of hot water until the sugar dissolves. Remove from heat and whisk until cold. An electric whisk saves the wrist!

3 Mix the creams together and whisk until they thicken slightly. Fold the cream into the egg mixture and add the oatmeal. Pour into a bowl and freeze overnight.

Petticoat Tails

(from Borders)

Shortbread, along with its various derivatives such as 'millionaires' with chocolate on the top, is popular throughout Scotland and many manufacturers make it with added ingredients such as ginger or chocolate chip. The best of these commercial brands is that made by the Edinburgh Shortbread Company, but here is an old recipe, originally from Meg Dod's *Cook and Housewife's Manual*, for a more delicate biscuit. It is allegedly called petticoat tails because the shape resembles the nineteenth-century petticoat hoops; it is also suggested that the name is a corruption of the French *petites gatelles*.

Makes 12
Preparation time: 1 hour

200g (7oz/1¾ cups) plain (all-purpose) flour, plus extra for dusting
50g (2oz/⅓ cup) icing (confectioners') sugar, plus extra for dusting

85g (3oz/⅓ cup) butter
25g (1oz/2 tbsp) lard

1 Preheat oven to 180°C (350°F/Gas 4).

2 Mix the flour with the icing (confectioners') sugar in a large bowl. Add the butter and lard and rub together until the mixture resembles fine breadcrumbs. Turn out on to a floured board and knead to a firm dough.

3 With a rolling pin, roll out a round about 0.5cm (¼ in) thick. Cut into 12 segments, slide them onto a baking sheet and bake for 20 minutes or until lightly brown. Remove from the oven and dust with icing (confectioners') sugar, then leave to cool.

Rhubarb Baked with Angelica

(from Fife)

This rhubarb recipe is another contribution from Monica Heyman's
recollections of her youth at Kellie Castle.

Serves 4
Preparation time: 1 hour 20 mins

700g (1¹/₂lb) young rhubarb   85g (3oz/¹/₃ cup) caster (superfine) sugar
5–7.5cm (2–3 in) fresh angelica stem, chopped

1   Preheat the oven to 150°C (300°F/Gas 2).

2   Chop the rhubarb in at least 2.5cm (1 in) long 'logs'. Place the rhubarb and angelica in a
    shallow baking dish and sprinkle with the sugar.

3   Cover with foil and bake in the oven for 1 hour. The sugar will draw out the juice of the
    rhubarb, keeping its shape, and the angelica will delicately complement the sharpness
    of the fruit.

Nutty Flapjacks

(from Borders)

Makes 12
Preparation time: 40 mins

225g (8oz/1 cup) butter   450g (1lb/5¹/₂ cups) rolled oats
225ml (8fl oz/1 cup) honey   115g (4oz/1 cup) chopped walnuts
175g (6oz/1 cup) dark soft brown sugar

1   Preheat the oven to 180°C (350°F/Gas 4).

2   Melt the butter with the honey and sugar in a large pan. Stir in the oats and walnuts and
    mix thoroughly.

3   Place in a 27.5 x 18cm (11 x 7 in) baking pan and smooth the top with a palette knife.
    Bake for about 20 minutes then cut into 12 fingers. Leave in the pan until completely
    cold before removing.

RHUBARB TARTS

(from Fife)

I love rhubarb. It has a long season, starting with the lovely tender pink shoots
that are ideal for this recipe and growing bigger later on, when it can be used
in fools, chutneys and jams. It is important to preheat the baking sheet here
because this allows the pastry to cook from the bottom as well as the top,
keeping it crisp.

Serves 4-6
Preparation time: 1 hour

225g (8oz) puff pastry
550g (1¼lb) rhubarb, washed and trimmed
115g (4oz/½ cup) caster (superfine) sugar

50g (2oz/⅓ cup) icing (confectioners') sugar
whipped cream, to serve

1   Roll out the pastry to 3mm (⅛ in) thick, and use a side plate to cut out a round. Then,
    with a saucer, press on the pastry to mark a border about 3mm (⅛ in) in from the edge.
    Cut as many rounds as you need, and freeze any excess pastry for another use.

2   Cut the rhubarb down the middle, and cut into pieces about 1cm (½ in) in length. Mix
    with just enough caster (superfine) sugar to coat and leave for at least 30 minutes, but
    no more than 2 hours, to 'sweat'. The sugar brings out the moisture, partly 'cooking' the
    fruit.

3   Preheat the oven to 220°C (425°F/Gas 7).

4   Put a baking sheet in the oven to heat; this allows the pastry to cook from the bottom as
    well as the top, keeping it crisp. Drain the rhubarb and spread over the pastry rounds
    within the border.

5   Carefully slide the pastry rounds onto the heated baking sheet and cook for 15 minutes.
    When cooked, the edges should be slightly browned and raised. Dust the tarts lightly
    with icing (confectioners') sugar, and serve on individual plates with whipped cream.

Selkirk Bannock

(from Borders)

A traditional sweet bread, very much of the Borders region.

Serves 6-8
Preparation time: 1 hour 30 mins

200g (7oz/1 cup) caster (superfine) sugar
425ml (15fl oz/scant 2 cups) milk
900g (2lb/5 cups) strong (bread) flour
pinch of salt
25g (1oz) fresh yeast or 2 tsp dried

115g (4oz/¹/₂ cup) butter
115g (4oz/¹/₂ cup) lard
450g (1lb/3 cups) sultanas
oil, for greasing

1 Dissolve 2 tsp of the sugar in a little of the milk, and keep aside for the glaze.

2 Put the flour with the salt in a warm place. Warm a little milk and add the yeast with a teaspoon of sugar. Leave to froth.

3 Melt the butter and lard with the remaining milk and keep warm. Add the yeast to the flour, and then add the milk and fat mixture. Mix until it forms stiff dough.

4 Knead the dough for a few minutes, then cover with a cloth or cling film (plastic wrap) until it doubles in size. Knock back, then knead in the sultanas and the rest of the sugar. Shape into 2 rounds. Put on to an oiled baking sheet and leave to rise in a warm place until about twice the size.

5 Preheat the oven to 220°C (425°F/Gas 7).

6 Bake in the oven for 10 minutes, then reduce heat to 190°C (375°F/Gas 5) and continue baking for another 15 minutes. Remove from the oven and coat the bannock with the glaze; return to the oven for a further 15 minutes.

STRAWBERRY PUDDING

(from Glasgow)

Not a hot pudding as the name might suggest, but a very simple chilled one, similar to a bavarois or any of the thickened milk-type puddings. The Italians would make it with cream and call it *panna cotta*! The base of a custard set with gelatine can be used for all sorts of fruits such as raspberries and brambles. With strawberries it's quite nice to have some slightly over-ripe so their colour blends through the custard, making it go pink! The best strawberries are the really small ones or the wild ones you can pick in the hedgerows. My father never really cared as much for strawberries as he did for raspberries, a taste I now agree with, but he did attempt to grow some alpine ones once which were excellent. I remember they were called Baron Solamacher – now that is a good name!

Serves 4
Preparation time: 40 mins + setting time

225ml (8fl oz/1 cup) milk
a few drops of vanilla essence (extract)
3 leaves gelatine
4 egg yolks

85g (3oz/¹⁄₃ cup) caster (superfine) sugar
250g (9oz/2 cups) strawberries, roughly cut up, plus extra (whole) for serving
225ml (8fl oz/1 cup) double (heavy) cream

1   In a large pan, scald the milk and add the vanilla. Soak the gelatine in cold water to soften.

2   Whisk the egg yolks and sugar together until pale, then pour over the hot milk and whisk in thoroughly.

3   Return the pan to a low heat and stir with a wooden spoon until it begins to thicken just like a custard. Remove from the heat, stir in the gelatine to dissolve, and then strain. Leave to cool.

4   When cool, add the strawberries as the mixture begins to set. Lightly whip the cream and fold into the mixture. Pour into a pudding basin and set in the refrigerator overnight.

5   To serve, warm the base of the bowl in hot water and turn out; serve with more strawberries.

GLASGOW

Glasgow has historically been the melting pot of Scotland, a great maritime city which has been influenced by cultures and tastes from many parts of the world. It was also a place where the very rich and the desperately poor lived cheek by jowl; a century ago the rich merchants were importing French chefs to add sophistication to their dining tables while the poor struggled to survive on bread and tea in the city's notorious slums. Today, Italian ice cream-makers cater to the traditionally sweet tooth of Glaswegians, Indian and Bangladeshi takeaways provide them with a taste of the exotic, while those who continue to enjoy one of their city's staples will still find plenty of fish and chip shops. Historically, Glasgow's taste has always favoured good, solid fare and, of all Scotland's regions, this is the place to come for puddings and pies.

One of the most interesting rooms in the Tenement House, belonging to The National Trust for Scotland, is the kitchen, preserved as it would have looked a hundred years ago.

One of the most fascinating places to visit in Glasgow is The Tenement House, a rare survivor of the many tenement buildings which were a major feature of the city right up to its post-war reconstruction. Now in the possession of The National Trust for Scotland, it is a perfectly preserved time capsule that allows visitors to get a first-hand impression of domestic life one hundred years ago. For over fifty years Miss Agnes Toward prepared meals for herself and, until her death, her invalid mother in the kitchen, with its coal-fired range and Victorian equipment and hoarded everything from theatre tickets to butcher's bills. Among the recipes, some clipped from magazines, others typed or handwritten, preserved in this unique archive is one for cooking haddock or whiting which reminds us of the days when the British middle classes (Miss Toward earned her living as a shorthand typist) still believed in the virtues of simple (in this case very simple) home-cooked food, as opposed to what they probably thought of as 'foreign muck'.

1 whiting · some butter · 2 plates · pepper and salt
A pan with some boiling water

Take scales off haddock, trim fins, turn head backwards, take it off. Slip the knife down inside close to the bone, take out the bone. Butter a dinner plate thickly, lay on the fish, skin side downwards, put a few pieces of butter on the fish, lay another plate on the top and place on the pan with the boiling water. Steam for twenty minutes and serve it on the hot plate it was cooked on.

Another of Miss Toward's recipes, this time from the dark days of rationing during the Second World War, is for 'creating' butter.

For 1lb butter beat together a quarter lb butter and quarter lb margarine. Slowly add one tablespoon dried milk reconstituted with milk. Warm small teacup of milk to blood heat. Add slowly and keep beating. This gives nearly 1lb of creamy butter and does not deteriorate.

Neither of these recipes encourages one to yearn for the 'good old days', but even then there were those who believed that traditional cooking could be improved upon. In a leaflet advertising 'The Waterless Cooker' (whatever became of that, I wonder!) I found the following homily from a Dr Forbes Ross:

Raw fruit and veg contain potassium, but the idiotic process of boiling vegetables in water instead of cooking them in their own juices, the eating of fine white bread, etc are among the causes of this large increase in cancer. It would be less foolish to throw away the veg and consume the water.

I am still not sure that this is a message some cooks have fully taken on board!

Summer Pudding

(from Fife)

Here is a reprint of a recipe found in the series of recipe books I have called the 'Malcolm recipes'. This one is a forerunner of what we now know as summer pudding, for which my own recipe follows; but, as you can see, any sort of fruit can be used.

Mary Douglas Malcolm's Fruit Pudding

Take a round pint or quart basin - line with bread about half an inch thick press it well in. Make some apple sauce (stewed and sweetened) which must be poured in while boiling hot, till the basin is filled. Lay a slice of bread on the top cut to size of the basin, wrap the basin in a thick cloth to keep stew in.

Make it the day before. Make a custard with 2 eggs and milk with a little sugar and bay leaf which when cold must be poured over. It may be made with rubarb (sic) or any other fruit.

Summer pudding to me is a part of what summer is all about, evocative of long warm days and laden fruit bushes. The luscious quality of the inside of the pudding, especially when eaten with cream whipped to perfection, is positively sensual.

Serves 4
Preparation time: 40 mins + chilling time

medium or thinly sliced crustless white bread
225g (8oz/1 1/2 cups) strawberries, halved
225g (8oz/1 1/2 cups) fresh seasonal fruit e.g.
  raspberries, cherries, brambles etc.

2 tablespoons water
150g (5oz/ 2/3 cup) caster (superfine) sugar
double (heavy) cream, to serve

1   Neatly line the base and sides of a 850ml (30fl oz/3 3/4 cup) pudding basin with the bread, cutting to fit where necessary.

2   Wash and trim or stone (pit) the fruit where necessary.

3   Put the water and the sugar into a pan and bring to the boil.

4   Add the fruit, the largest and firmest first (i.e. cherries, strawberries, then raspberries etc.) and cook briefly, ensuring that they still hold their shape. Drain off the syrup and reserve.

5   Spoon the fruit into the prepared bowl and cover with more bread, then spoon over a little of the syrup. Put a saucer on top and weight it. Refrigerate overnight.

6   Turn out the pudding, cut into wedges, and serve with the remaining syrup poured over and a blob of lightly whipped double (heavy) cream.

TEA LOAF/FRUIT CAKE

(from Borders)

Once again a traditional kind of tea bread or fruit loaf. It must have originally
come from Edinburgh, because they would always have had tea left in the pot,
whereas Glaswegians would have generously given it all away!

Serves 6
Preparation time: 1 hour 15 mins

450g (1lb/3 cups) dried fruit
225g (8oz/1 ½ cups) soft brown sugar
200ml (7fl oz/scant 1 cup) cold tea

450g (1lb/4 cups) self-raising flour
1 tsp ground mixed spice
1 egg, beaten

1   Preheat the oven to 190°C (375°F/Gas 5) and line a loaf pan with greaseproof (waxed) paper.

2   Mix the fruit and brown sugar together in a large bowl, add the tea and soak overnight.

3   Add the flour, mixed spice and beaten egg. Pour the mixture into the lined loaf pan and
    bake for 45-50 minutes. It is cooked when a skewer inserted comes out clean.

ZABAGLIONE

(from Fife)

Another dish enjoyed by the Crichton Stuarts at Falkland Place

Serves 4
Preparation time: 40 mins

4 egg yolks
4 tbsp caster (superfine) sugar
1 tbsp warm water

7 tbsp sweet Marsala
sponge fingers (ladyfingers), to serve

1   Place the egg yolks, sugar and warm water in a bowl over a saucepan of hot water. Beat
    with a balloon or rotary whisk (not an electric beater) until pale in colour and frothy.

2   Whisk in the Marsala, a little at a time, and continue whisking over heat until the
    mixture increases in volume, becomes thick and foamy and holds its shape in a spoon –
    about 5-10 minutes.

3   Remove from the heat immediately and spoon into tall wine glasses. Serve with sponge
    fingers (ladyfingers).

SWEET PASTRY FOR FRUIT TARTS

(from Dumfries)

The essential pastry for all pastry-based puddings. It can be used for simple biscuits as well and flavoured according to need by adding a teaspoon of cinnamon or some grated lemon zest, vanilla essence, etc.

Makes enough pastry to make 2 x 20cm (8 in) flan cases
Preparation time: 2 hours 30 mins

150g (5oz/^{1}/$_2$ cup plus 2 tbsp) butter
50g (2oz/^{2}/$_3$ cup) caster (superfine) sugar

225g (8oz/2 cups) plain (all-purpose) flour, plus extra for dusting
1 egg

1 Cream the butter and sugar together in a food processor; add the flour and mix to form a breadcrumb mixture, then add the egg and whiz until it begins to form a ball. Do not overmix. Leave in a cool place for 1 hour before use.

2 Roll out the pastry, using plenty of flour to dust the work surface. Make sure the size is right, then roll the pastry around the rolling pin and place it over the tart pan and unroll it over the pan. Press down gently.

3 Leave to chill for 1 hour then bake it blind. Preheat the oven to 190°C (375°F/Gas 5). Line the flan case with cling film (plastic wrap) then fill with dried beans or ceramic pie weights and bake in the oven for 20 minutes until the pastry has 'set'. It will just be going light brown at edges.

4 Remove the pie from the oven, and lift out the cling film (plastic wrap) with the beans. Retain the beans for future use. Return the flan case to the oven to dry out, but take care not to burn the top. Once cooked, leave to cool.

5 For fruit tarts, just spread a layer of pastry cream inside and cover with fruit of your choice!

TAYBERRY TART

(from Fife)

Unique to Scotland, this wonderful fruit is really only good if the summer is
hot enough to ensure that it ripens properly; if it is not then it's best made into
a lusciously scented jam or perhaps a fool (see Groser Fool on page 134). This
tart combines the best of ripe Scottish fruit with the traditional French tart.
Although they wouldn't have been made with tayberries in her day, Mary,
Queen of Scots will certainly have enjoyed such tarts at Falkland Palace or
Myres Castle.

Serves 4
Preparation time: 1 hour

225g (8oz) sweet pastry (see page 148)
115–175g (4–6oz/³/₄–1 cup) tayberries
icing (confectioners') sugar, for dusting

For the pastry cream:
425ml (15fl oz/scant 2 cups) milk
5 egg yolks
175g (6oz/³/₄ cup) caster (superfine) sugar
few drops vanilla essence (extract)
70g (2¹/₂ oz/¹/₂ cup plus 2 tbsp) plain (all-
purpose) flour

1   Line a 20cm (8 in) tart pan with the pastry and leave it in a cool place for 1 hour. Preheat
the oven to 200°C (400°F/Gas 6) then bake the flan case blind in the oven for about 15
minutes. Leave to cool.

2   Meanwhile, make the pastry cream. Scald the milk in a pan, taking care not to let it
burn. In a bowl, beat the egg yolks with the sugar until pale, then beat in the vanilla.
Whisk in the flour until smooth and continue whisking while you pour in the hot milk.
Whisk until it is all combined, return to the pan and, over a low heat, stir with a wooden
spoon until the mixture thickens. Remove from the heat and allow to cool. [In a bowl,
covered with greaseproof (waxed) paper or cling film (plastic wrap), this will keep in
the refrigerator for 1 week.]

3   Spread pastry cream over the base of the flan to a depth of about 3mm (¹/₈ in). Wipe the
tayberries and push the stalk end gently into the pastry cream, starting at the edge, and in
a circular pattern, fill the whole tart. Just before serving, dust with icing sugar.

WHOLEMEAL BREAD

(from Aberdeen)

Where do you start with bread? There have been entire books written on the subject, but I felt it necessary to include at least one recipe. This one is based on the original Grant Loaf, created by Doris Grant in the 1950s as the best sort of wholemeal loaf.

Doris Grant came to address a conference of Scottish Women's Guilds in Aberdeen and, while staying with my parents, came down with a cold. She was furious because she never got ill, and was determined that no one should know that the great Doris Grant had a cold! My parents thought it all very amusing. This is the bread my mother has made ever since.

Makes 3 loaves
Preparation time: 1 hour + time to prove

1.5kg (3lb 4oz/9¹/₂ cups) wholemeal flour
2 tsp salt
3 tsp dried yeast

3 tsp brown sugar or honey
750ml (27fl oz/3¹/₃ cups) warm water
oil, for greasing

Note: This a very basic wholemeal brown loaf; it is quite solid but full of flavour. If you prefer a lighter texture use some ordinary brown flour mixed with the wholemeal.

1   Put the flour in a large bowl with the salt and leave in a warm place.

2   Meanwhile, put the yeast and sugar or honey in a jug and about 150ml (5fl oz/²/₃ cup) of the warm water. Mix to dissolve. Leave in a warm place, with a cloth over the top, until the yeast begins to froth - about 10 minutes.

3   Prepare 3 bread tins by greasing them thoroughly. Warm them in the oven briefly.

4   When the yeast is ready, pour onto the flour and mix in. Add the remaining warm water, mix well and then knead by hand or in a mixer with a dough hook. The texture should be moist but should not stick to your hands.

5   Divide the dough into 3 and press into the tins. Cover with a cloth and put in a warm place to rise. The loaves should double in size.

6   Preheat the oven to 200°C (400°F/Gas 6) and bake for about 35-40 minutes.

PRESERVES,
SAUCES,
AND
DRINKS

MARMALADE

(from Aberdeen)

Often traditionally thought to have come from Dundee, the story goes that in the early eighteenth century a Spanish ship carrying what we would now term Seville oranges put into Aberdeen harbour due to heavy winds, The perishable cargo was made available for sale and bought by James Keiller who could not resist a bargain (must have been an Aberdonian!). It was his wife who had to sort out what to do with the problem of the near rotting fruit and came up with what we know today. However, the word 'marmolet' had been in use since the sixteenth century and indeed Shakespeare makes mention of Seville oranges in his punning line given to Beatrice in *Much Ado About Nothing*, 'Civil as an Orange'.

Makes about 1kg (2lb)
Preparation time: 2 hours

1kg (2lb) Seville oranges
2 lemons

2.5 litres (80fl oz/10 cups) water
1.8kg (4lb/8 cups) granulated sugar

1   Wash the fruit, leave it whole and place in a large pan. Add the water and bring to the boil; simmer for about 1 hour until you can easily pierce the fruit. Remove the fruit from the pan, reserving the liquid.

2   When the fruit is cool enough to handle cut it into slices, whatever thickness you like; traditionally it was thick cut. (Alternatively, whiz the fruit in a food processor for a minute, if you prefer small chunks of fruit which are easy to manage on toast.)

3   Remove the pips and return them to the water and simmer for another 10 minutes, then strain the liquid into a preserving pan. Add the chopped fruit to the preserving pan, add the sugar, bring to the boil and simmer rapidly to setting point.

4   Transfer to sterilized jars and seal.

Tartare Sauce

(from Aberdeen)

Makes about 175ml (6fl oz/³/₄ cup)
Preparation time: 20 mins

150ml (5fl oz/²/₃ cup)
mayonnaise
2 tsp chopped capers

2 tsp chopped gherkins
2 tsp chopped fresh parsley
1 tsp chopped fresh tarragon

1 tsp chopped fresh chervil
juice of ¹/₂ lemon

1   Mix all the ingredients together and allow about 1 hour to marry the flavours before
    serving – excellent with grilled fish or fish cakes.

Mushroom Ketchup

(from Borders)

Wild mushrooms make the best ketchup of all and adding it to soups, sauces, stews etc.
can make a big difference. This recipe is much as the one on page 130 but takes less time!

Preparation time: 6 hours + 2-3 days macerating

mushrooms, wild or cultivated
salt

For the spice mix:
3 cloves garlic, chopped
1 red chilli, deseeded and chopped
1 tsp allspice

¹/₂ tsp grated nutmeg
¹/₂ tsp ground ginger
300ml (10fl oz/1¹/₄ cups) red
   wine

1   For every 450g (1lb) of mushrooms you will need 1 tbsp of salt. Break up the mushrooms
    into small pieces and layer them in a large bowl with the salt. Leave for 2 or 3 days to
    sweat out the juices, and give them a press every so often to help the process.

2   Preheat the oven to 110°C (225°F/Gas ¹/₄) and put the bowl of mushrooms in the oven for
    3 hours to get the last drops of juice out (an Aga is ideal for this). Strain through a nylon
    sieve, squeezing as much juice out as possible, and then measure the mushroom liquor.

3   For every 1 litre (44fl oz/5¹/₂ cups) of liquor, allow 1 quantity of the spice mix. Add this
    to the mushroom liquor and simmer gently for 2 or 3 hours, then strain into sterilized
    bottles. The result will keep for some months and is excellent in place of ketchup or as
    an addition to stews etc.

TOMATO SALSA

(from Edinburgh)

This one is also delicious as an accompaniment with grilled food or salads. You should always remember: with good Scottish produce you don't need much to set it off!

Serves 4
Preparation time: 40 mins

6 ripe tomatoes
zest of 1 lemon
zest of 1 lime
1 tbsp chopped fresh parsley
1 tbsp chopped fresh coriander (cilantro)

1 clove garlic, finely chopped
1cm (½ in) piece fresh ginger, peeled and diced
2 tsp balsamic vinegar
2 tbsp olive oil

1   Blanch and peel the tomatoes by plunging them into boiling water for 10 seconds, then plunging them into cold water. Remove from the water and peel, then cut them into quarters and remove the seeds. Cut each quarter into small strips and then into small dice.

2   Combine with all the other ingredients, finishing with the olive oil.

SALSA VERDE

(from Edinburgh)

In effect a green sauce, fabulous with fish or grilled chicken.

Serves 4
Preparation time: 20 mins

85g (3oz/1½ cups) chopped fresh flat-leaf
   (Italian) parsley
70g (2½oz/1¼ cups) chopped fresh mint
50g (2oz/1 cup) chopped fresh tarragon
4 tbsp capers

4 tsp Dijon mustard
3 cloves garlic, crushed
50g (2oz) canned anchovies
juice of 1 lemon
6 tbsp extra-virgin olive oil

1   Put everything except the oil into the processor and whiz until it purées, then stir in the oil and that's it!

ONION RELISH

(from Glasgow)

Something of a modern idea this, but slow-cooked onions are delicious, whether for a relish or as a 'marmalade'. This goes well in tarts or as an accompaniment to cheese dishes or a base to flans. Here is a basic relish.

Makes about 225g (8oz)
Preparation time: 50 mins

85g (3oz/^{1}/$_3$ cup) butter
2 large onions, peeled and finely chopped
4 tbsp white wine

4 tbsp red wine vinegar
1 tbsp honey
1 tsp soy sauce

1 Melt the butter in a large frying pan and fry the onions until soft and lightly brown stirring frequently – about 20 minutes.

2 Add the remaining ingredients and cook gently for another 20 minutes until the mixture has thickened slightly – it should have a lovely dark unctuous quality.

SKIRLIE

(from Glasgow)

Such simplicity but such a good gravy soaker-upper! This traditional accompaniment to roast meats is also very good as a stuffing for birds (chicken or turkey) or in stuffed tomatoes as a side dish.

Serves 8 as an accompaniment to roast meat
Preparation time: 40 mins

115g (4oz/^{1}/$_2$ cup) dripping (drippings) or lard
2 onions, peeled and finely chopped

175g (6oz/1^1/$_4$ cups) medium oatmeal
salt and freshly ground black pepper

1 Melt the dripping (drippings) or lard in a large pan and sweat the onions in it until soft. Add the oatmeal and continue to stir until golden brown – about 10 minutes; season to taste.

2 Serve as a traditional accompaniment to roast meats. It is also very good as a stuffing for chicken or turkey, or to stuff tomatoes as a side dish.

Tomato Chutney

(from Dumfries)

This is a hot, spicy chutney making use of both ripe and green fruits. It should be kept for a few months before using. Warning: The cooking fumes are very strong, so work in a well-ventilated kitchen when you make it! But it is worth it.

Makes about 2 kg (4½ lb)
Preparation time: 30 mins + cooking time

1kg (2lb) each red and green tomatoes
2 tsp fenugreek seeds
3 tbsp coriander seeds
2 litres (70fl oz/9 cups) malt vinegar
450g (1lb) onions, peeled and chopped
450g (1lb/3 cups) raisins
450g (1lb/3 cups) soft brown sugar

1 head garlic, peeled and chopped
100g (4oz/½ cup) capers
4 tbsp salt
1 tbsp cayenne pepper
1 tsp crushed cardamom pods
1 tsp ground nutmeg
1 tsp chopped fresh basil

1　Chop the tomatoes roughly or whiz them quickly in a food processor.

2　Roast the fenugreek and coriander together for a few minutes in the oven or in a dry pan, then grind them either in a mortar and pestle or crush them with the end of a rolling pin.

3　Cook the tomatoes in half the vinegar over a low heat until the mixture thickens, taking care that it does not burn.

4　Pour the remaining vinegar into a large pan and add the fenugreek and coriander mixture and all the remaining ingredients. Cook until the onions are soft. Add the tomato mixture and simmer together for 10 minutes. Place in sterilized jars and cover.

NECTAR – A SUMMER DRINK

(from Borders)

Here is another recipe from Mary Malcolm.

Put 1 lb sugar 2lb raisins chopped or whole and 2 lemons peeled and sliced into a cask. Pour theron 2 gallons of boiling water ... Stir the whole well. Once every day for 4 or 5 days then strain and bottle it will be fit for use in 9 or 10 days

ELDERFLOWER CHAMPAGNE

(from Borders)

Makes about 7 litres (250fl oz)
Preparation time: 15 mins + 24 hours soaking + fermenting time

4 heads of elderflowers gathered in full
sunshine to avoid excess moisture
1.35kg (3lb/6 cups) granulated sugar

4 tbsp white wine vinegar
9.5 litres (335fl oz/42 cups) water
2 lemons, cut in half

1 Find a clean bucket which you can cover (a cloth will do) or a plastic barrel from a beer-making kit. Put the elderflowers, sugar, vinegar and water in it and squeeze the lemon halves into the mixture; cover. Leave for 24 hours and then strain.

2 Pour into plastic bottles leaving at least 2.5cm (1 in) of space at the top. Seal the bottles and leave for about 2 weeks in a cool place. Fermentation takes place and the result is a delightful sparkling, refreshing drink.

Do not use glass bottles because there is a risk of one exploding! Not a pleasant experience.

Bibliography

The following are books which I have used specifically and in my research.

Geddes, Olive, *Lairds Larder*, HMSO/The National Library of Scotland
Grigson, Jane, *Jane Grigson's Good Things*, Penguin Cookery Library
Hartley, Dorothy, *Food in England*, Little, Brown
Kapoor, Sybil, *Modern British Food*, Penguin Cookery Library
Lady Castlehill's Recipe Book, Molendinar Press
Lady Maclean's Cookbook, Collins
Lawrence, Sue, *Sue Lawrence's Scottish Kitchen*, Headline
McNeill, F. Marian, *Scots Kitchen: Its Traditions and Lore with Old-time Recipes*, Blackie
Robert Gordon's Technical College and Aberdeen School of Domestic Science,
    The Aberdeen Cookery Book, Aberdeen Press and Journal
The Cook's Cook Book, Robert Hale

Other writers who have inspired my writing include Catherine Brown, Richard Olney, Nichola Fletcher, Mary Contini, Elizabeth David, C Anne Wilson, Nigel Slater, Simon Hopkinson, Marco Pierre White and Theodora Fitzgibbon.

Suppliers

R. R. Spink and Sons, Sir William Smith Road, Kirkton Industrial Estate, Arbroath, DD11 3RD. 01241 872023. **Arbroath Smokies.**

Summer Isles Foods, Achiltibuie, near Ullapool. 01854 622 353. www.summerislesfoods.com. **Distinctive smoked salmon, some organic.**

Keracher Fishmonger, 73 South Street, St Andrews. 01334 472 541; 56 Scott Street, Perth, 01738 638 454. www.keracher.com. **Stocks a wide variety of fresh fish.**

Loch Fyne Oysters, Clachan, Cairndow, Argyll, PA 26 8BL. 01499 600264. www.loch-fyne.com. **First class smoked and fresh fish and oysters.**

Salar Smokehouse Ltd, Lochcanarnan, South Uist. 01870 610 324. www.salar.co.uk. **I believe the best flaky smoked salmon comes from here.**

Ramsay of Carluke, 22 Mount Stewart Street, Carluke, ML8 5ED. 01555 772277. www.ramsayofcarluke.co.uk. **Dry-cured bacon.**

Puddledub Pork, Tom Mitchell, Clentrie Farm, Auchtertool, Kirkcaldy, KY2 5XG. tomclentrie@aol.com. **Dry-cured bacon and gammon.**

Fletchers of Auchtermuchty, Reediehill, Auchtermuchty, Fife, KY14 7HS. 01337 828369. www.fletcherscotland.co.uk. **Farmed venison, 'veniburgers' and pies.**

Ramsay of Carluke, Wellriggs, 22 Mount Stewart Street, Carluke, ML8 5ED. 01555 772277. www.wellriggs.demon.co.uk. **A superb traditional butchers, with particularly fine dry-cured bacon.**

Rannoch Smokery, Kinloch Rannoch, Near Pitlochry, PH16 5QD. 01882 632344. www.rannochsmokery.co.uk. **The only smokery in Scotland to supply smoked wild venison, as well as many other smoked products.**

Macbeth the Butcher, 11 Tolbooth Street, Forres, Moray, IB36 OPH. 01309 672 254. macbeths@lineone.net. **Superb quality beef from Highland and Aberdeen Angus herds.**

Macsween Haggis Specialist, Dryden Road, Bilston Glen, Loanhead, Edinburgh, EH20 9LZ. 0131 440 2555. www.macsween.co.uk. **They offer a complete Burns Supper by mail order, including their excellent haggis.**

Iain Mellis, 30a Victoria Street, Edinburgh, EH1 2JW. 0131 226 6215; 492 Great Western Road, Glasgow, G12 8EW. 0141 339 8998; 149 South Street, St Andrews, KY16 9UN. 01334 471410. **Cheesemonger.**

Island Cheese Company, Home Farm, Brodick, Isle of Arran. 01770 302 788. **Bellevue blue and goats crottins.**

Isle of Mull Cheese, Sgriob-Ruadh Farm, Tobermory, Isle of Mull. 01688 302 235. www.isleofmullcheese.co.uk. **A fabulous cheddar-type cheese.**

Valvona and Crolla, 19 Elm Row, Edinburgh, EH7 4AA. www.valvonacrolla.com. **This is a top quality deli.**

Jamesfield Organic Farm, Abernethy, Perthshire. 01738 850 498. www.jamesfieldfarm.co.uk . **A full range of organic food from meat to vegetables.**

Heather Ale Ltd, Craigmill, Strathaven, Lanarkshire, ML10 6PB. **A wide range of excellent beers.**

The Oatmeal of Alford, Montgarrie Mill by Alford, Aberdeenshire, AB33 8AP. 01975 562209. **Oatmeal.**

Scotherbs, Kingswell, Longforgen, Dundee, DD2 5HJ. 01382 360642. **Cut fresh herbs are available from here all year round.**

Eassie Asparagus, Sandy and Heather Pattullo, Eassie Farm, Eassie, Forfar, DD8 1SG. 01307 840303. **Asparagus.**

INDEX